'Katy Lees has produced an excellent book to assist trans people with their mental health. Their easy-to-read guide includes straightforward information about various theoretical models and approaches, with useful strategies, tips, and techniques to aid readers to manage challenges such as self-harm, shame, depression, trauma, and much more.'

– Dr Jos Twist, clinical psychologist

'We're living through a tough time indeed – particularly for trans folk – and most of us are feeling the toll it's taking on our mental health. Katy Lees provides just the kind of friendly voice, and helping hand, we need at such times, reminding us why we're struggling, and helping us to find what will work for get us through the hardest moments, whatever form those take. With plenty of practical suggestions and a lot of kindness, this book is just the resource trans people need right now.'

– Meg-John Barker, author of *Hell Yeah Self-Care!*

'I wish someone had handed me this book ten years ago. In compassionate, accessible language Lees sets down what it takes many trans people decades to find out: that we are unique, valuable, and loved, and it does get better. I can already tell that this book's lucid, practical advice is going to help so many people – I can't wait to recommend it to everyone I know!'

– Eris Young, author of *They/Them/Their*

'This is such a useful book, looking at the mental health struggles of trans people in both a systemic and a personal way, with flexible and creative approaches to self-care and a very community-based conceptualization of healing. The book doesn't flinch away from how hard it is being trans in the UK right and looking closely at the ways

T0015591

can be impacted. I appreciate that it doesn't give easy answers but still creates a wealth of resources. The self-disclosure of the author also humanizes the book and gives it a vibe of "we are all struggling with this, here's a few things that can help", which makes it affirming and encouraging without being patronizing. There is also an incredible resource list at the end of the book and a practical guide to seeking therapy and other forms of help.'

– Sam Hope, author of *Person-Centred Counselling*
for Trans and Gender Diverse People

'This straightforward, accessible book is a great guide to techniques that you can use to improve your mental health even if you don't have access to counselling or support. It addresses key issues facing trans and non-binary people with clarity and understanding, explaining how common they are and what you can do to feel better. Do try this at home.'

– Jennie Kermode, author

'This book contains everything I wish my younger non-binary self had known. As a trans elder and experienced psychotherapist, Katy shares just the right balance of information about mental health, practical tips, and personal insight to support trans people in navigating this complex issue. The supportive and nurturing tone of the book made me feel as though Katy was walking alongside me. Every trans person (and those wanting to support trans people) should read it!'

– Gem Kennedy, transformational practitioner, activist,
and founder of Queers & Co. podcast

THE TRANS GUIDE
TO MENTAL HEALTH
AND WELL-BEING

of related interest

The Anxiety Book for Trans People
How to Conquer Your Dysphoria, Worry Less and Find Joy
Freiya Benson
ISBN 978 1 78775 223 8
eISBN 978 1 78775 224 5

Yes, You Are Trans Enough
My Transition from Self-Loathing to Self-Love
Mia Violet
ISBN 978 1 78592 315 9
eISBN 978 1 78450 628 5

Trans Power
Own Your Gender
Juno Roche
ISBN 978 1 78775 019 7
eISBN 978 1 78775 020 3

The Trans Self-Care Workbook
A Coloring Book and Journal for Trans and Non-Binary People
Theo Lorenz
ISBN 978 1 78775 343 3
eISBN 978 1 78775 344 0

The Trans Guide to Mental Health and Well-Being

Katy Lees

Jessica Kingsley Publishers
London and Philadelphia

First published in Great Britain in 2022 by Jessica Kingsley Publishers
An imprint of Hodder & Stoughton Ltd
An Hachette Company

1

Trigger Warning: This book mentions anxiety, eating disorders, self-harm, substance abuse, suicide, trauma and transphobia.

A CIP catalogue record for this title is available from the British Library and the Library of Congress

ISBN 978 1 78775 526 0
eISBN 978 1 78775 527 7

Printed and bound in Great Britain by TJ Books Limited

Jessica Kingsley Publishers' policy is to use papers that are natural, renewable and recyclable products and made from wood grown in sustainable forests. The logging and manufacturing processes are expected to conform to the environmental regulations of the country of origin.

Jessica Kingsley Publishers
Carmelite House
50 Victoria Embankment
London EC4Y 0DZ

www.jkp.com

Contents

Acknowledgements

I want to start by thanking my kind, courageous, and brilliant fiancée, Lucy, who patiently waited for me (and on me) while I spent evenings and weekends writing this book. She gave me erudite and caring opinions about what to include, gifted me advice and wisdom, cheered me on, cheered me up, and made me endless cups of coffee. I love you, Lucy – thank you for loving me!

Next, I want to thank Andrew James, Emily Badger, Isabel Martin, Victoria Peters, and Bonnie Craig at Jessica Kingsley Publishers, who made the process of getting this book out into the world so much smoother and kinder than I ever thought it would be. Andrew, Emily, Isabel, Victoria, and Bonnie – thank you for being an excellent team.

This book got its start because of Michelle Snow from the What The Trans!? podcast. Michelle deserves all kinds of accolades and gratitude for the amazing work she does, but I want to thank her specifically for initially giving me the voice that I used again to help people with this book. Michelle – thank you for helping me speak up about trans mental health.

There are also the people who currently look after my

mental health, who deserve more gratitude than I could ever convey. First is Gem Kennedy, a wonderful coach who has helped me to move forward, follow my actualizing tendency, and quieten my inner critic as I worked on creating this book (and as I learned to take my own self-care advice!). Gem – thank you for helping me grow. Then there's Jessica Cadbury, a fantastic HAES-focused nutritional therapist, who has helped me to be kind to my body and mind, something that you'll see echoed in the spirit of this book. Jessica – thank you for helping me to find my energy.

I want to thank everyone at Sherwood Psychotherapy Training Institute (SPTI) who supported my therapy training, from the dedicated tutors Michelle Oldale, Michelle Addison Raven, and Ambika Erin Connelly, to every amazing student that I met while I was there. So many of you are my friends now, and all of you have helped me to be the person, and the therapist, that I am today. SPTI friends – thank you for the congruence, empathy, and unconditional positive regard.

Last but not least (but definitely the most clichéd), I'd like to thank my family. Over the 18 months it took me to write this book, my mum, Christine, and my step-dad, David, provided everything I needed to keep me strong and stable, while my sisters – Mattie, Cara, and Cacilia – have given me all kinds of laughter and light. There are also my niblings – Alexander, Felicity, Scarlett, Brianna, Freya-May, and Caleb-John – who remind me that the future is bright. Thank you, all, for being my foundation.

Hello, You!

Hello! I'm so glad you're here! I'm pleased that you have found this good mental health guide for transgender and/or non-binary people. My hope is that this guide will set out advice and strategies on a range of common mental health issues for trans people who are struggling with their mental health, whether they are simply looking for ways to improve their lives or are in crisis. It should be helpful no matter your gender or stage of transition, or even if you decide not to transition in conventional ways. You can read this front-to-back or dip in when you need to – hopefully, you can work with this book in whatever way works best for you to get your needs met.

I know first-hand how difficult it can be to find affirming and effective mental health care when you are trans and/or non-binary, and I would like this book to provide that for you. You deserve to have an informative book that can help you gain self-love, self-care, and self-empowerment. Trans people deserve good mental health care that helps them feel better in the short- and long-term (including – especially – you), provided by someone who actually knows what they are talking about (including – optimistically – me).

Together we'll be exploring many of the challenges faced by many trans people, such as working through the highs and lows of change, examining how gender dysphoria and gender euphoria affect how you feel about yourself more generally, and investigating the trauma of stigma from family members and the outside world. The book features evidence-based and well-tested psychotherapeutic advice, including my own experiences as a therapist and as someone who has experienced mental illness, with explanations of therapeutic terms and experiences.

This guide was written from a person-centred perspective and by a person-centred psychotherapist. The person-centred approach is a humanistic style of counselling pioneered by Carl Rogers in the 1940s that championed an egalitarian relationship between the counselling client and the counsellor, where the counsellor helps the client to follow their actualizing tendency and begin their journey to 'the good life' (Rogers 1961). This might sound intellectually fancy but it essentially means that person-centred therapists are trained to help people be who they really are and who they really want to be, beyond who they have been told they 'should' be. A person-centred approach recognizes: that differences are to be celebrated; that what works for some people might not work for others; that self-compassion and self-understanding are as important as the compassion and understanding we have for others; and that everyone has the potential to be almost anything they want to be. I will also talk about other mental illness and mental wellness theories and strategies from different modalities but, wherever the path of wellness might take us, we will be sticking to a person-centred framework of safety, self-love, self-respect, understanding, acceptance, openness, honesty, and reaching your very individual sense of fulfilment. Perhaps the most important thing to remember here is that you can make a change, and that change is about what brings you euphoria in your life and in your gender.

Let's begin, together!

A Bit About Me

A Bit of a Biography

I am Katy Lees, a non-binary, person-centred therapist and writer. I use they/them/their pronouns.

I first came out to myself as non-binary when I was about 19, and then to someone else as non-binary when I was 21, during the early days of my MSc in Person-Centred and Experiential Psychotherapy. Even though some of my earliest memories centre my feelings around my gender, it took me a while to figure out exactly what being non-binary meant for me, and to realize there was a word for people who felt the way I did. I experience euphoria and dysphoria around my gender and presentation, although I don't think a person has to experience either of those things to be transgender or non-binary. While some non-binary people don't identify as transgender – which is very valid – I do identify as trans, simply for the reason that I was not assigned non-binary at birth. Because of this, you may see me refer to 'trans' people in general in this book, by which I mean anyone who is not cis, or anyone who does not fully feel like the gender they were assigned at birth all the time. If you're a non-binary person who does not identify as transgender, you are valid and I am still referring to you!

It is also worth noting the axes and intersections of my experiences of oppression and privilege. I believe it's important to touch on this so that you can understand the lenses through which I view the world as a therapist and as a trans person. I am a white, British, queer, non-binary person of size, who is currently in my early thirties. I experience chronic physical illness, I am neurodivergent, and, although I consider myself to be mentally well right now, I am still living with the consequences of experiencing long-term trauma and mental illness. I grew up middle class in a working-class city in the north-east of England and, according to The Great British Class Calculator (BBC 2013), I am currently an emergent service worker. I am transmasculine and often misgendered by strangers. I asked my partner to describe how others might perceive my gender, and she described me as a 'hard-femme butch', which I think is pretty accurate.

I have worked in mental health services for my whole adult life in various positions, including: as a nursing auxiliary for people with Huntington's disease in the NHS; as a senior care worker for people with challenging aspects of dementia for DUFA; as a counsellor in several mental health charities across the Midlands and the north of England; and now in my own private psychotherapy practice, where I put my BSc in Psychology and my MSc in Person-Centred and Experiential Psychotherapy to good use. A good many of my service users and clients over the years have been members of the LGBTQ+ community and I have helped clients of many different genders along the way, much to my pleasure and interest. In my current private practice as a therapist, almost all of my clients are part of the trans community, and many are also otherwise queer, polyamorous, neurodivergent, and survivors of trauma.

My Experience of Mental Illness and Recovery

I have been working on my own mental health for much of the time period in which I've been working as a therapist. I first had therapy with a secondary school counsellor, returned to see a private therapist at 21 when I began my therapy training, and I've always had some kind of therapy or coaching since then. Through most of this time, I've been reckoning with anxiety and low self-esteem, two issues that I am always improving on and working with. Recovery there is a slow and lifelong process that I am happy to be undertaking. While most of my experience with both mental ill health and recovery have been chronic, this has not always been the case.

When I was in my mid-twenties, I had what I can only describe as a complete mental breakdown. I was working a full-time minimum-wage job in mental health care, volunteering as a counsellor with survivors of sexual abuse, working several side hustles to pay for my therapy training, trying to process a breakup and worsening chronic physical health problems, and trying to write my MSc dissertation, all at the same time. With all of this going on, plus the stress and trauma I had experienced over the previous 20 years of my life, something inside of me just broke. I stopped feeling emotions. I stopped feeling connected to myself or my life. I stopped eating, drinking, and sleeping. All I could do was go to work; all of my other time was spent lying on a mattress on the floor and staring at the walls. I had panic attacks whenever I left my bed and periods of depersonalization so intense that I couldn't speak. It felt like someone had scooped out all of the good, functional, kind parts of me and left a sea of boiling mud in its place – and I felt that if I ever opened my mouth to ask for help or be honest about what a mess I was in, all of that mud would come oozing up onto the poor hypothetical person who had innocently asked me how I was, flooding my life forever.

In the moments when my head felt less foggy, I tried to figure out what to do. I'd been working in mental health for my whole adult life, and I had years of therapy training and clinical experience under my belt – I felt I should have known what to do to help myself. Every element of self-care and recovery I could think of was so emotionally hard or practically difficult that everything felt impossible. I was exhausted and my executive function – the part of me that knew what I had to do every day and sectioned off the energy to help me do it – was completely dysfunctional. Even brushing my teeth or washing my face felt impossible on most days.

Eventually, I had to make the agonizing decision to start doing the impossible. I went to my doctor and I told them how I felt, resigned to the knowledge that I might be either dismissed or sectioned, and was treated with both kindness and medication. For the first time, I opened up to my therapist (who I was seeing for a very reduced price after admitting I couldn't really afford to be there) about how awful I was feeling and got more of the therapeutic support I needed. I told my tutors at university what was happening and, after a lifetime of forcing myself to be a perfect student, finally admitted that I was failing. I opened up to family, to friends, to colleagues, to my support system at large, and nobody drowned in the muddy anger and sadness that came pouring out of me. Most people wanted to help me, and I found I could deal with the people who didn't. Eventually, I felt well enough to make the most impossible decisions of all, the ones I had desperately needed to make for my own safety but had thought I would never be able to make without catastrophic consequences – I stopped volunteering as a therapist for a while, I took my dissertation year again, I quit my full-time job, and I moved out of the mouse-infested house that I was struggling to rent by myself to live with a new partner (who's now my fiancée). A support network I hadn't realized was there caught me and made sure I wasn't homeless and starving, as I had assumed I would be if I took this leap. I allowed myself to do something I didn't think I deserved – I rested for a while, I talked honestly about how I felt, I started to meet my needs and let other people meet them, and I healed.

Now, in my thirties, I feel happy and calm for the first time in my life. I have a thriving therapy practice and I love my job. I talk honestly about my feelings, with professionals and my community, every day. I take the time to rest, to play, and to check in with what I need. I make sure the things I know will help me are accessible to me. Life isn't perfect, but I trust myself to meet my needs, and caring for myself no longer feels impossible. I've made it through to a place where I can address the ups and downs of life in healthy ways, including by taking medication and talking things out with professionals if that's what I need. Even so, I think I'm going to be a little weird, a little jumpy, and a little anxious for life – these things get baked into the delicious cake of your personality over time. I still take my anti-depressants and anti-anxiety medicines because they still help and, even though I feel the best I've ever felt, I'm still very open to the idea that life can get even better. Right now I live a good life (Rogers 1961) with plenty of fulfilling work, supportive loved ones, loud laughter, and quiet calm – a life that I've had to teach myself is possible for someone like me, and a life that I feel is possible for you, too.

You Might Be Like Me

It felt important to tell you my story to show that you're not alone. Like 40% of non-binary people (Valentine 2016), I have experienced a long-term mental health issue, and like 66% of all trans people (Ellis, Bailey, and McNeil 2015), I have made use of private, government-funded, and NHS mental health services. The trauma that contributed to my period of acute emotional distress was often related to my internally felt and externally perceived queerness, leading to adult diagnoses of anxiety, depression, and complex post-traumatic stress, with all the accompanying panic attacks, insomnia, dissociation, disordered eating, chronic fatigue, hypervigilance, executive dysfunction, and generally terrible times that tend to go with these things. One of the reasons I feel so much better now is because I am also in a safe space where I can express my queerness and my gender and be met with joy and understanding from the people around me, something that I've seen repeated in my clients over and over.

Transgender people like me are often going through mental ill health; 84% of trans people have expressed suicidal ideation, for example, with 55% being diagnosed with depression (McNeil et al. 2012). This should be no great surprise; when people try to understand and express who they are in a globally hostile environment, while also experiencing discomfort about many aspects of how they perceive themselves and how they are perceived by others, it's no wonder that this can lead to experiences of prolonged sadness, anger, anxiety, hopelessness, and any number of long-standing feelings related to trauma.

Even though I've recovered from my breakdown, recovery is a process that I am still engaged in and learning about, especially as I find new ways to express my trans identity and new understandings of what that means in the world around me. Healing, as they say, is not linear. I've discussed my gender identity with my fair share of therapists myself, and they've ranged from the supportive, to the kindly befuddled, to the outright transphobic. Those interactions have pushed me to understand what a trans person such as myself might need to work towards good mental health, whether they have sought out therapy to discuss their trans identity or not.

If you're a trans and/or non-binary person who's looking to improve your mental health in any way, this is for you!

My Experience of Being a Trans Person-Centred Therapist

When I started training as a person-centred therapist, I was a freshly hatched babytrans, straight out of my bachelor's degree, and the youngest person on my course. I'd wanted to be a therapist for basically my whole life (and also a writer and an astronaut – two out of three ain't bad!), and I was excited to make a difference.

I was particularly drawn to the person-centred approach because of its humanism and its guiding principle of an equal relationship between the practitioner and the client. Each individual's thoughts and feelings are understood as unique and every client is seen as the expert in their own experience, allowing the client to take control of their life with the help of an enriching, compassionate, and respectful relationship with their therapist. In this way, a person's actualizing tendency – their desire to grow in all ways to reach their full potential – is nourished by the therapist providing three essential therapy elements, known as the core conditions. These are congruence (the therapist knows how they're feeling and is genuinely them-selves with the client), unconditional positive regard (respect for the client without judgement) and empathy (understanding how the client feels) (Mearns and Thorne 2000). When the client and the therapist work together in a safe relationship to get the client where they need to be, the client is supported and under-stood enough to grow and thrive (Rogers 1957). This modality seemed optimistic while still being realistic, and it encouraged non-directivity from practitioners in order to help clients get to where they wanted to be, not where they were supposed to be, an attribute that I really valued as a queer, fat, neurodivergent person who was trying to work out the intricacies of their gender.

About ten years and thousands of therapy hours later, I'm now one of the few out trans therapists I know, and I'm still excited to make a difference. I have a full caseload of clients, almost all of whom are trans and/or non-binary. Although I've faced some transphobia from trainers, other therapists, clients, and strangers alike, I feel lucky that I can help some of the most vulnerable and amazing people I've ever met. Practising as a person-centred therapist still feels right to me, and I hope you can see why this theory works particularly well for trans, non-binary, and gender non-conforming people through its leading presence in this book.

Self-Care

In this chapter, we'll explore issues like the different kinds of self-care that might work for you, new ways to address your needs as a trans and/or non-binary person, caring activities you can do for yourself, finding self-care in your community, and why self-care is much more than just a buzzword.

What Is Self-Care?

The concept of self-care can be difficult to pin down for some people. There has been a capitalistic movement towards implementing 'self-care' as a buzzword that can be used to sell face masks, detoxes, and expensive retreats, meaning true self-care can feel unattainable if you don't have much disposable income.

Self-care, in essence, is ensuring you have what you need. Sometimes, that's definitely taking some time off for a bubble bath and a face mask, but often it involves making sure you're doing what you need to do, even if it feels difficult or uncomfortable. Self-care can be meeting your basic physical needs, like: getting enough to eat and drink; pursuing hobbies that interest you; ensuring you have enough human contact to suit your needs and personality; and seeking out aspects of spirituality, education, and self-expression (Maslow 1943; Cross 2007; Blackstock 2011).

As you read the self-care tips in this chapter, try to remember that self-care isn't something you need to deserve or something you need to earn. You don't need to have done a certain amount of work to 'indulge' in it, and you don't need to be feeling bad, tired, or ill to rest. Self-care is sometimes about recovery, but it doesn't always have to be; self-care is still important when you're feeling happy and well. No matter what you think you've earned, you deserve rest, breaks, food, comfort, company, and so much more. Taking care of yourself is absolutely essential to your mental health.

It's also worth remembering as you read through this section of the book, and as you take in any other self-care advice, that these things may not work for you. Different people benefit from different help at different times (Cooper and Dryden 2015), and self-care is not something that you can pass or fail. If something here doesn't help you, that's okay, and you're okay! It doesn't mean you've done self-care wrong or that you're not trying hard enough; it just means that particular idea isn't working for you right now. There will be other ways to care for yourself and many more ideas to try.

The Good Life as a Transition

One way that Carl Rogers writes about self-care and the pursuit of happiness is in the development of a 'good life' (Rogers 1961). The good life, to Rogers, is less about finding the ultimate best way to live your life, and more about finding open and caring ways of engaging with self-care. In this way, caring for yourself is less about trying to find that perfect state of bliss, but more about staying compassionately curious about your changing needs and trying hard to meet them. Rogers was careful to state that this ideal of the good life is not a destination but a process and a direction (Rogers *et al.* 1967). In this way, caring for yourself is about going forwards instead of trying to stay still. You could even call ongoing self-care a transition in itself.

According to Rogers in his 1961 work, *On Becoming a Person: A therapist's view of psychotherapy*, there are three qualities to foster in yourself if you want to engage in the process of living your own good life.

- *An increasing openness to experience.* This is about being fully accepting of every experience that comes from within you or outside of you, and processing everything without defence mechanisms or cognitive distortion. This involves being able to listen to your thoughts and emotions without judgement or dissociation, including pain, fear, anger, and grief, but also including courage, hope, awe, and love. This is a tall order, and I don't think anybody truly gets to a stage of total openness to experience, but remember that it's the journey that matters and not the destination. Any self-care that you can do to be with your feelings, thoughts, and experiences more fully is going to improve your life.

- *Increasingly existential living.* This is about living each moment in the present, something that today we might call mindfulness. It comes with an understanding that your self – your thoughts, feelings, personality, and actions – comes from what you are experiencing, and not the other way round. Understanding that life happens to you, instead of trying to fit your ideas of life around how you think it should be, allows you to actively participate in the world and change it. Working on self-care that gets you closer to this line of thinking can help you to be adaptable, resilient, and open to experience.

- *An increasing trust in your organism.* This is about learning to understand and trust your ability to care for yourself. The more you can fully accept what you're thinking, feeling, intuiting, and experiencing, the easier it should be to be able to meet your own needs. In this way, you can function more fully as yourself and truly give yourself what you need in the moment. Trusting in yourself allows you to know you can handle what existential living and an openness to experience can throw at you. Any self-care that helps you to feel safe, listen to yourself, and meet your own needs will be helpful in this.

Rogers hypothesized that a person who is open to as many experiences as they can be, living in the moment as opposed to worried about the future or grieving for the past, and trusting themselves to meet their own needs, will be more able to grow in the direction that they need to be, and become, their true self. The aim here is not to be a perfect embodiment of mindful competence – everybody dissociates, everybody worries, everybody grieves, and everybody doubts themselves sometimes – but to transition in your life and self in ways that help you love yourself, see the world, care for yourself, and change for the better.

Your Hierarchy of Needs

Maslow (1943) popularized the idea of self-care as essential to all kinds of growth with his theory known as Maslow's Hierarchy of Needs. In this hierarchy there are several steps, with your basic physical needs at the ground level, followed by literal and emotional safety, enjoyment of life, and self-actualization, which is the sense that you're going where you'd like to be going in life. The theory argues that if our basic needs are not being met, it is difficult for us to meet our other needs, causing physical illness and emotional distress. It is important to remember, in this case, that self-care can come in layers, and that treating yourself to luxuries is going to be less effective in a world where you are not always safe or secure. This is unfortunately true for many trans people (Bachmann, Gooch, and Long 2018; Speegle 2020), and so your more basic needs, such as food, warmth, and your felt sense of safety, may need to be more of a priority to you than more privileged wellness-seekers might have you believe. This is not to say that you should leave your spirituality, education, emotional growth, and self-expression at the wayside – in fact, caring for ourselves with these things can be a literal lifesaver (Cross 2007; Blackstock 2011). This is more to say that, before you treat yourself to your well-deserved face mask, it's worth asking yourself – have you eaten enough today? Have you had enough sleep? Have you communicated with a loved one today for an amount of time that made you feel comforted and happy? Are you in a safe environment and, if not, is there anything you can do to make yourself safer? And, if it speaks to you, have you offered yourself a little treat like a bath bomb or a favourite food without feeling that you need to earn it?

Self-Care Comes in Degrees

As well as hierarchies, there are degrees to self-care. It's tempting to think of self-care in terms of black and white or good and bad, but this can be an unhelpful way of thinking that encourages you to give up altogether. It's okay if your self-care comes in degrees and if you sometimes struggle to take care of yourself in 'big' ways, because anything that you can do is enough.

Take a relatively simple task that tends to fall by the wayside when people feel low on energy and resources – brushing your teeth. Sometimes, it's really difficult to find the energy to do this less-than-exciting chore twice a day, especially if your self-esteem is low or other things seem more important. Obviously, it's best for your dental hygiene if you brush your teeth for two minutes twice a day, and you know that, but that doesn't stop it from being difficult to commit to when you're anxious, stressed, or depressed. When you're low on resources – the energy needed to get to the bathroom, for example, or the money to buy good toothpaste – it's tempting to just stop brushing your teeth altogether, causing an array of problems later. If you can't brush your teeth for two minutes twice a day, it's important to remember that you have not failed if you only brush for one minute, or once a day, or if you can only rinse your mouth out with water, because any of those things help more than not brushing your teeth at all. If you just can't find the resources to do any of that, this is also not a failure on your part, as it means you are saving your resources for other things you need. If you need to just focus on breathing right now, and save brushing your teeth for another day, then that's alright.

When Self-Care, and Everything Else, Is Really Difficult

Sometimes, you might find yourself feeling so bad that you literally can't do anything. Your days are spent in bed, or barely being aware of your surroundings at work, or doing nothing but crying on the sofa.

Caring for yourself as best you can when you don't have any motivation to do loving things for yourself also counts as self-care. Self-care is doing what you need to do with the resources that you have. My advice is to go at your own pace and do the things you feel you want to do when you feel you can. It's not your fault if you can't find the energy for big acts of self-care. Anything you can do is enough. With this in mind, there are plenty of things you can try to do to take care of yourself if you are struggling with even getting out of bed.

My greatest self-tested trick is to use any spare energy you might have one day to make the next few days as easy as possible. If you usually struggle to get out of bed during the day to get food and drink, for example, use your extra minute of energy one day to make sure you have bottles of your favourite soft drinks and easy-to-eat, long-lasting snacks by your bedside. The next day that you can't face going to the kitchen for lunch, your food and drink will be within arm's reach. Other helpful things can be kept close by in case of a catastrophic loss of motivation or physical ability, too: a pile of fresh blankets stacked nearby can help when your duvet is full of crumbs and you can't bear to change it; hand sanitizer, face wipes, deodorant, and water wipes are better than nothing at helping you feel fresh when you can't face the dysphoria and hard work of a good shower. Keeping little stashes of essentials around the house where you usually like to hang out can also mean you get all the essentials you need even if you're stuck in one place, which can hopefully mean you have the energy to feel better a little sooner. Make things as easy, accessible, and stress-free for yourself as you can.

Now is also very much the time to ask for help from anyone around you. The people around you – whether they're friends, family, members of your community, or professionals – will almost certainly be glad to help you. If you can, getting in touch with people to ask for specific things you need will be easier for you and for them – people, in general, like to know exactly how they can help. The help you ask for can be anything you need, for example help to get food, to pick up your medicine, to keep your space tidy, to get in touch with professional services, to watch your children, to remind you to eat, even just to talk at a certain day or time.

While you're struggling with taking care of yourself, it's worth holding on to the idea that anything you can do right now is okay. Don't worry about whether or not you should be doing more. Beating yourself up for not caring for yourself robs you of the energy you need to care for yourself. You're doing great!

Self-Care When It Feels Like You're Starting from Scratch

When you've reached a point where you can do a little more to take care of yourself, you may find that you need some extra resources to fully take care of yourself. You may feel like you're starting from scratch and that you need to get your necessary self-care needs taken care of. There are several ways you can seek self-care when you feel like you're starting from the beginning but you're able to face the world a little more.

If at all possible, get your basic healthcare seen to as soon as possible. Schedule a visit to your doctor to discuss your mood, your sleep, and your energy levels. If you're attending a gender identity clinic, ask if they can refer you to a therapist who works with trans people. Get a dental check-up. Go to the opticians. If at all possible, and if you live in England, apply for an HC2 or HC3 certificate to help with the medical costs – as of early 2020, if you're earning under £16,000 a year, you can get a great deal of your NHS treatment for free with these certificates, including necessary dental care and help with costs at the opticians, and you can still receive some help if you're earning over this amount. You can also get extra help if you're receiving certain benefits, so it's worth spending a little energy to investigate what help you can get. If you live in America, make use of any medical insurance you have.

It can be really, really difficult to find anything fun, interesting, or emotionally nutritious to focus on when you're struggling, so I recommend starting small. Find a low-stakes activity that you enjoy and stick with it for as long as you enjoy it. This could be anything manageable and enjoyable, like listening to music, watching TV, playing video games, listening to podcasts, being in your garden, going for walks – anything that's accessible for you that doesn't take more energy or resources than you have. Find small things that bring you glimmers (Dana 2018) of peace or contentment. If happiness seems far off, look for the moments in your day where you feel the least awful, and try to think about what you can healthily replicate from the experience. When it doesn't feel good any more, it's okay to stop. Remember that stopping when something starts to feel bad – or the fact that it feels bad at all – is not failure. It just means it's not serving you right now and it's time to do something else instead. If you're struggling to find joy in an old activity but you don't want to give it up, try to find a new way to engage in the activity that reroutes around the source of the problem. If you love to read, for example, but you are not able to concentrate on the act of reading, audiobooks and podcasts are a less hands-on way to enjoy stories. If dressing in ways that make you feel gender euphoria used to get you through hard times but now you're not in a safe place to do so, find a trusted friend to keep your wardrobe safe in another place and play with gender-affirming scents, accessories, and styling if it's safe to do so. It's okay to find joy or comfort in something for a short while and, if it doesn't serve you any more, stop when it isn't useful and try something else. If something only makes you feel good for a little while, it doesn't mean you have failed at it or that your recovery isn't going well. It's normal to need to switch things up.

What Makes You Feel Good?

As difficult as it might be to think about, it is worth gently examining what brings you good feelings. It's a good idea to approach this with a compassionate curiosity – sometimes you'll find that the things that bring you a reprieve from bad feelings aren't very good for you, for example, or you won't know of anything that makes you feel good at all. It's okay to explore the feelings that come with those thoughts and keep gently questioning yourself.

If the things that make you happy are unhealthy, maybe ask yourself what activities help you to feel healthier, instead, depending on your understanding of what 'health' means to you. This could include making sure you're eating enough, spending some time outside, and stretching gently. Chances are, if something feels truly healthy to you, there's a little joy to be found there when you're able to see it.

To explore what makes you feel good right now, it's okay to try as many activities as your energy and concentration will allow. These activities can be low or high energy, social or solitary, loud or quiet, inside or outside, calm or exciting, creative or sedentary. Spend some time thinking about anything that pops into your head when you think about feeling good, and give it a try if you can. Take a look at the things happening in your life that make you feel the least bad, and try to make more time for them.

As you try more things and access little slices of happiness, it will be easier to figure out which activities feel best to you and which categories of activities you might need right now. For example, if you find yourself feeling better when you watch TV, spend a moment thinking about the experience – do you prefer to watch TV alone or with others? Do you like long action movies, bingeable horror series, or low-stakes cartoons? Do you like TV shows where you can switch off your brain a little or TV shows that you have to really pay attention to? When you know why something feels particularly good to you, it can be easier to find more of the same.

If nothing much makes you happy or healthy, what brings you comfort or security? What gives you energy or makes you feel at peace? Which friends, family members, or social groups make you feel the most safe when you get in contact with them? What makes you feel less tired, less numb, or less anxious? You may not have answers to all of these questions yet, which is not a bad thing. You may already know the answers to these questions but not have the resources to act on them as much as you'd like, or you may have no idea what you can do that would feel safe and growthful. There is always time to find things that suit you – there is always much more time than you think there is. Sometimes, focusing on harm prevention instead of happiness is all that you will have the emotional room for. There will be time for other things later, I promise.

Guilty Pleasures

Your self-care activities don't have to be anything traditionally healing. If the stereotypes of yoga, meditation, and journaling don't fit with you, you don't have to do them. If your ideas of comfort, relaxation, and rejuvenation are really off the beaten track, it's still okay to go for it. For example (so you don't feel alone), for some reason, something that helps me feel normal again after a period of intense emotion is wrapping myself in a huge blanket nest while wearing my onesie that makes me look like a wolf and eating grated cheese out of the bag. It's weird, but it does the job of making me feel like an actual person again when I emerge from my fleece-and-cheese cocoon.

Likewise, if that stereotype of self-care where you listen to low-fi music and meditate is all you want and need, please don't be ashamed that it's a stereotype – do whatever helps. Taking time to participate in a guided meditate, write in my journal, and take a hot bubble bath can certainly help me to feel more calm and resilient after a stressful week. Trust your mind and your body, and go with what feels helpful. Self-care activities can include anything that makes you feel a little better than you felt before. You never have to feel guilty for your guilty pleasures!

Exercising as Self-Care

I know you've heard this one before, but bear with me! Moving in ways that you're able to, and in ways that make you feel happy, are so good for self-care. The key to this kind of self-care will be finding something that genuinely feels good to you, and not doing the kind of exercise you think you 'should' be doing. If it hurts, emotionally or physically, you don't have to exercise in this way – or at all, if this doesn't work for you!

I also recognize that exercise can be difficult to do safely; the changing rooms at the gym can be extremely intimidating, for example, as can exercising comfortably outside if you're anxious about being misgendered or catcalled. Not only this, but trying to go from 0 to 60 on a training programme can be actively bad for your mental and physical health. It may be best to start slow, small, and at home or with a trusted friend, and to follow some light yoga or stretching videos online.

Gentle stretching and balance-based exercises that get your heart beating – like yoga, walking, cycling, or low-impact circuits – have proven to be especially good for grounding your brain and body, especially in terms of improving your emotional self-regulation and resilience (van der Kolk *et al.* 2014; Fetzner and Asmundson 2015; Rhodes, Spinazzola, and van der Kolk 2016; Sullivan *et al.* 2018). These exercises are also relatively easy to practise and build on at home or in safe areas. There are trans-friendly, weight-neutral, accessible resources for exercise you can do at home, like the book *Yoga for Everyone* by Dianne Bondy (a Black, plus-size cis woman and yoga teacher) or online workout videos from *Decolonizing Fitness* by Ilya Parker (a fat, Black, non-binary physical therapist). If you feel comfortable leaving the house, a gentle walk in a calm space with someone who makes you feel safe can help you to connect with your body and the outside world. The goal is to stretch and move as you are able and at your leisure, so walking outside can look any way you want, from a stroll in your local park where you can often stop to look at foliage and cool bugs, to a brisk walk on the beach, all the way up to a spirited hike up a mountain trail.

If you wear a binder, please remember to take a break from wearing one while you exercise and wear a sports bra instead. I know how dysphoric it can be to exercise without your binder, so, if a sports bra doesn't do it for you, try a low-impact exercise where you know you'll be able to breathe well and deeply, either while binding or just letting your chest be unbound under a baggy workout t-shirt.

If you usually tuck, it is also worth not doing so when you exercise, as you could be at risk of short-term and long-term pain and injury. Compression shorts designed for running or cycling worn under baggy workout clothes might help you to feel less dysphoric.

Positive Self-Talk

Another idea that might be helpful is to directly challenge any negative self-talk going on in your internal monologue (the voice most of us have in our heads that talks through the day). Having to listen to others bad mouth you can be exhausting and painful, so it stands to reason that listening to your own thoughts turn to self-criticism will also rob you of energy. It may be a difficult thing to pay attention to at first; negative self-talk can be loud and all-encompassing or it can be the quiet little voice in your head that insults you when you drop something. Try to pay attention to when negative self-talk occurs, in your head or out loud, even if it comes in the form of self-deprecating humour.

When you find yourself thinking a negative thought about yourself, saying that comment out loud, or apologizing for a small mistake or something you didn't do, stop and take a deep breath. Let that breath out slowly. Take a gentle, curious, compassionate look at the words – what do they really mean? What was the emotion behind the words? Maybe you were frustrated that you made a mistake, annoyed that you made a joke that didn't land well with other people, or sad that your new clothes aren't as gender-affirming as you thought they'd be. Take another deep breath and let it out slowly. It's okay to feel the way that you feel about what happened. Try to flip the thought around to something neutral or even positive, if you can. *Everybody makes mistakes and I can fix this one*, for example. Or, *I still think the joke is funny! The right people will love that joke. I wonder what other jokes I know that can make these people laugh*. Or, *those clothes don't fit me in a way that makes me feel good and that's not my body's fault. I can return those clothes and find something that makes me feel really good*.

If your negative self-talk sneaks out into the world disguised as self-deprecating humour, it's important to know that, even if it's meant as a joke, you're still hearing yourself saying mean things about yourself. Try some silly self-aggrandizement instead – for example, if like me you tend to accidentally drop your rubbish on the floor instead of in the bin, even when the bin is directly in front of you, making jokes about how you meant to slam-dunk that wrapper onto the floor like the pro basketball player you are is both healthier and funnier than any self-deprecating joke you can make.

Community-Based Self-Care

Connection is very important to our continued well-being (Broadhead *et al.* 1983). Not only is community a source of joy, comfort, and information, but we're wired to seek out social co-regulation for our thoughts and emotions (Dana 2020) – that means most of us like to process how we're feeling with others in some way. While caring for yourself is obviously your top priority, I also think it's worth considering self-care as a part of community care, and vice versa. As I said at the beginning of this chapter, capitalism would love to see us treat self-care as something we do alone after spending money on products, and it doesn't have to be. Having safe, positive social relationships of all kinds can greatly improve our health in so many ways (Cacioppo and Cacioppo 2014) and help us feel that our lives are meaningful (Stillman *et al.* 2009). Being with others that we trust can be an excellent source of self-care, and caring for ourselves in the community is an important part of looking after ourselves.

Finding a sense of community can be difficult for many trans people. Seeking family, friends, romance, and interest-based communities can activate really big feelings about conn-ection, rejection, and protection (Dana 2020), especially when we habitually feel unsafe in relation to others (Porges and Carter 2017). In light of this, maybe you can take a moment to think about how your support system (the people you like and feel safe with who help you through tough times) looks right now. Are these people family, friends, partners, support workers, community groups, healthcare professionals, online groups, colleagues, peers, authority figures, acquaintances? Are they other trans people, connected to the LGBTQ+ community, or allocishet (as in alloromantic, cisgender, and heterosexual)? Who feels safe in your support system? How does your body feel when you think of each individual? Which of these people offer support, connection, rest, joyful activity, or a combination? Are there people in your support network that understand the 'real you'? Are there connections that feel particularly safe, supportive, and happy, or any that aren't meeting your needs? Is there anything else you feel you need? There are no wrong ways to find and build a community, but having an idea of who is in your life right now can be an excellent way to explore what you need.

It's okay to meet your needs by letting people take care of you while you look after yourself. This is especially true if your mental health is suffering right now. Behaving in this way can feel uncomfortable for many people – independence and being able to take care of yourself is seen as very important in Western society, and taking resources such as time and money from others can cause us to feel useless and guilty – but no matter how you feel about yourself right now and how you feel about asking for help, you deserve the things you want and need and it's okay to ask for them. Seek out the help that you can afford, whether you're paying for private childcare while you take a break from parenting or accessing free support groups in your area to talk about how you feel. Take as much help as you can get with costs, education, therapy, furniture, food, heating – anything that anyone is offering. Take what is offered for as long as you can bear it.

When you're well enough – genuinely well enough, with energy and resources to spare – you can take part in further community care by sharing your own skills to the best of your ability. It can be great self-care to look after others in your community in ways that take less energy but that still have a big impact. Making small but regular donations to those in need, particularly people who are in more vulnerable community groups than you, can mean so much to them and make you feel reaffirmed and reconnected. If you're a white person, saving what you can for a monthly reparation fund and donating directly to Black trans women can be a great way of making a difference. Otherwise, you can pay forward the resources that people offered by offering what you can safely spare.

Depending on your levels of energy, physical wellness, mobility, money, and other resources, you might also begin to think about the things you enjoy and how you can help others in your community by sharing what you love. This might involve spending a few hours a month volunteering at your local food-bank (which is great if you like to chat with people), sending a pen-pal letter every month to a trans person in prison (which is great if you enjoy writing snail mail and getting a bit arty – try the Bent Bars project), or checking in with your neighbours to see if they need anything.

Practising Resilience

Due to the stress of transphobia and existing as a member of a minority group, trans and/or non-binary people often need to be resilient in ways that cis people don't (Meyer 2015). The burden of this stress, from feeling like you don't easily fit in to being threatened with violence, adds up over time. To help you to carry the encumbrance of some of this stress, and to help you bounce back when you face trauma, you can practise resilience.

There are many different ways that queer resilience might look (Singh 2018), including the following.

- *Intrapersonal resilience*, e.g. taking care of yourself, which might look like challenging your negative thoughts about yourself and other trans people, affirming your physical self, discovering what makes you feel hopeful for the future, and working to fully embrace who you are.

- *Interpersonal resilience*, e.g. reaching out for support, which might look like telling yourself and other trans people that we are worthy, learning to ask for appropriate help, standing up to transphobic behaviour when it is safe to do so, or asking trusted individuals for advice.

- *Community resilience*, e.g. being part of a group of people that understands you, which might look like engaging in social justice, giving back and paying it forward when you have extra resources, or joining a support group to help yourself and others like you.

A big part of building your resilience as a trans person comes from getting to know who you are and what you need, and working out which messages that you're receiving from others help you to grow and which are designed to bring you down (Singh 2018). When do you feel most resilient and when do you feel you're growing most as a trans person? What, and who, makes you feel supported in your growth as a person? What inspires you? Seek out these experiences! What messages make you feel stuck, trapped, stagnant, or unsafe? Try to limit engaging with these messages when you can.

As important as I feel resilience is when you face oppression, I want to make it clear that I do not think this should be your responsibility. While it's important to be resilient, you shouldn't *have* to be – we should not live in a world where you have to practise resilience to get by. While continuing to practise resilience, and if you have the resources, I also think it's worth joining with others to try to create a society of fairness and justice so we do not have to be especially resilient in the future.

Self-Care and Media

Another way to care for yourself, particularly as a trans person, is to think about the type of media you consume. Over half of trans people report that the way trans people are treated by the media impacts how they see themselves (McNeil *et al.* 2012) and, with so much media portraying trans people in a negative light, it's worth considering if this is true for you and the media you take in.

Social media, for example, can have a surprisingly big impact on how you feel. You may find yourself 'doomscrolling', for example, or obsessively refreshing social media and news feeds looking for bad news or people to block. This can be a particularly potent compulsion when transphobia is in the news or, for example, if a celebrity you once trusted has revealed themselves to be a transphobe. It can be impossible to look away – who knows what piece of legislation that keeps us safe will be scrapped next or what formerly kind and influential voice is going to say they want to hurt us? It is important to strive for balance. Being informed about what's happening can combat a sense of isolation that I've noticed trans people can be particularly susceptible to, but continuing to look at something that upsets you after you have done everything about it that you reasonably can right now is a form of self-harm. Try to take breaks and to focus your social media attention on people, interests, and groups that help you feel safe, gently challenged, and ultimately understood. Block liberally when you come across accounts that feel harmful.

If you can, search for media (and not just social media) that includes people and characters that share your experiences. Find Instagram models who look like you, Twitter friends who share your pronouns, movies that embrace diversity, TV shows with trans casts and characters, and books about people like you loving and being loved. Take in as much trans media as you can that makes you feel seen, appreciated, and respected (Wallace 2018).

It is also important to remember that, when others are publicly anti-trans, this is not trans people's fault, and it is definitely not yours. You haven't done anything bad and you don't deserve any hatred for being who you are. It's transphobic people who are wrong, not you.

You can find out more about how to care for yourself in the face of traumatic media in the *Trauma* chapter of this book.

Transition-Focused Self-Care

One of the best ways to engage in healthy safe-care is to follow your euphoria. Choose the parts of transition, and of life, that feel good, even if they're difficult. The trick to it, in my experience, is to commit to loving who you are now and to loving whoever you will be – or, as Carl Rogers said, 'The curious paradox is that when I accept myself just as I am, then I can change' (Rogers 1961, p.17). For example, even if you feel like you don't deserve nourishment today, in the present you need to eat, and future-more-transitioned-you will need you to take care of yourself so they can exist. What can you do today to look after as many parts of yourself as you can?

Self-care while you wait for changes may also be an important part of your trans identity, at least for a while. Especially in the UK, where we face staggering waiting times to see NHS professionals at gender identity clinics, there are many parts of trans life that involve long waits that you can do little about. You will probably find yourself, or have already found yourself, waiting for appointments with a gender identity clinic, waiting for surgeries or procedures to take place, waiting for changes in your body if you take hormone replacement therapy (HRT), and even waiting for society to become more accepting. This waiting may take up more time in your life than is comfortable. There is almost always a way that you can make changes during those waiting periods, but the original wait may remain. It can be really frustrating, scary, and depressing to have to wait for changes that feel so immediately needed, and good self-care during these times can be essential.

You will change. This is a fact of both transition – whatever that means for you – and of life. It's okay to explore the things that give you energy and comfort while you wait for changes and transitions to happen.

This also applies to your transition. I know that the concept of 'transition' looks different for every trans and/or non-binary person, so here I use the word to mean 'anything that makes you feel closer to your own internal sense of gender'. This can include changing how you present yourself, seeking medical transition, changing your name, using certain pronouns, engaging in certain communities, trying on different labels, finding a song that really speaks to your gendered (or agender) sense of self, finding a pair of gender-affirming glasses that feel very 'you' – anything that makes you feel that little *zing* of self-recognition or *sigh* of calm. You may feel that this period of transition ends at a certain point, at which time you have fully transitioned, or you may feel that you will continue to transition forever. Neither of these feelings are wrong.

With transitions of all kinds come changes, both fast and slow, and you may have to engage in a lot of self-care as you go through any kind of gender transition. Transitioning in itself can be seen as self-care. Even when change is as positive as transitioning, it may bring all kinds of strong feelings that may be difficult to deal with. It's important to check in with yourself as much as possible through the process and with any trusted friends and family that are willing to lend an ear. Seeking professional therapy with a knowledgeable counsellor may also be helpful as you process the positive, negative, and neutral changes that your transition brings to light. You can read more about how to find a trans-friendly counsellor in the *There's Help Out There* chapter of this book.

All kinds of emotions and changes can be part of your progress through life and transition as you aim towards better mental health. Whatever small thing you can do for yourself in the moment, or whatever change you can make for a future version of yourself, can make all the difference (Johnson 2015).

Trauma

In this chapter, we'll explore issues like different kinds of trauma, why oppression is so traumatic, what the short-term and long-term effects of trauma can feel like, and how to work on feeling safe in a traumatic world that often includes transphobic media, family, laws, and strangers.

What Is Trauma?

Psychological trauma is the emotionally and cognitively painful damage that occurs when a person faces overwhelming powerlessness and stress. This trauma overpowers our coping mechanisms and hurts us in a way that we cannot control or find rational meaning in. Trauma usually threatens your sense of control, bodily integrity, sense of self, or your life itself (Herman 1992).

There are lots of different kinds of trauma (van der Kolk 2000). Some are obvious and well known, such as domestic violence, sexual abuse, or surviving war. People tend to think of trauma as one big, life-changing, hugely painful event, such as a car accident, surviving an attack, or losing a loved one, and all of these are excellent examples of trauma. These are sometimes known as 'big T' traumas.

Trauma can also include the build-up of less obvious and more insidious types of pain, such as being bullied, living with a chronic illness, and living in an unsafe environment. Others are less talked about but just as important, like grieving for a pet, breakups, seeing other people get hurt, dealing with oppression, long-term exhaustion, chronic pain, being repeatedly shamed for who you are, living in poverty, prolonged loneliness and isolation, and never feeling seen or heard. These are all kinds of trauma, and these particular types of trauma can be known as 'little t' traumas.

This is also why so many trans people seem to live with, and survive, trauma – all of these kinds of trauma are more common for people like us. In the UK and America, approximately two in five trans people have reported facing violent actions and threats (McNeil *et al.* 2012; FRA 2012; FRA 2020), with two thirds reporting discrimination and harassment (FRA 2012; FRA 2020) and one in five describing themselves as having been 'beaten up' (McNeil *et al.* 2012); 36% of trans people reported feeling discriminated against at work (FRA 2012; FRA 2020), a percentage which is only increasing over the years (FRA 2020); 14% reported being harassed by the police (McNeil *et al.* 2012); and two thirds of trans people believe the government does not effectively protect them (FRA 2020). Because of this, 60% of trans people are not open with others about their identity and experiences (FRA 2020).

All of these experiences can be highly traumatic. In fact, most trans people report surviving an act of discrimination that has majorly affected their quality of life (Grant *et al.* 2011). If you've gone through any of these traumatic experiences, or any not mentioned here, you are not alone and you can work through it.

In summary, trauma is any experience that psychologically, emotionally, or physically damages you, and trans people as a group tend to experience a higher amount of psychological damage than cis people.

A Note About Trauma and Your Trans Identity

I feel that it is important to state clearly that trauma does not make people trans. I have had a number of clients who have been in the relatively early stages of figuring out their gender who have asked me, 'What if I'm only trans because something bad happened to me? What if my dysphoria is just a delusion brought on by past trauma?' All of those clients worked out that this was not the case – that this was often misinformation given to them by people who wanted to hurt them. The Gender Critical movement in particular has often cited this as a truth in order to hurt and discredit trans people (Schevers 2021a; Snow 2021a).

There is no credible evidence to show that trauma, misadventure, or any illness, mental or otherwise, causes people to be transgender. What makes people trans is multifaceted, foundational, and complicated, like most things about being human, but trauma likely plays no part in this natural shaping. You are just wonderfully and wholly you.

The Web Model

The web model is a way of viewing minority stress and additional issues as highly relational (Hope 2019). The more oppression a person faces, the fewer social threads connect them to other people. For example, when a white person like me meets a white stranger, a neutral-to-positive social interaction is more likely to occur based on the other person's positive association with my skin tone, and a solid thread is built between us. As a non-binary person meeting a cisgender person, however, I am likely to be unthinkingly misgendered if the stranger is kind or deliberately mistreated if the stranger is transphobic, forming a broken thread between us. The more you experience oppression, the more of these broken threads are formed between you and your community. These cut social threads lead to further oppression in the form of the oppressed: becoming invisible, hypervisible, or both at the same time; being unable to access services and government benefits; having less access to employment, housing, and healthcare; being demonized and blamed for the poor treatment they receive; and being more likely to be assaulted, abused, and exploited.

The good news is that this means we can build especially strong social threads with the other trans people in our community, something that's been shown to be an excellent source of strength and comfort when you're dealing with trauma and oppression (Jackson Levin *et al.* 2020; Dana 2020; Seebohm *et al.* 2013; Buczynski and Porges 2012).

The Trauma of Oppression

As the web model shows, oppression, such as transphobia, and especially transmisogyny and transmisogynoir, can lead to several types of trauma and social exclusion. There's the cumulative effect of common aspects of the trans and/or non-binary experience, such as feeling generally unsafe, living with unjust laws, functioning through dysphoria, and having to be around unsafe people. Transphobia can also lead to large, single incidents of trauma, such as being attacked for being trans or being denied care by medical staff when seeking treatment in an emergency. These are all external events rooted in prejudice, also known as distal stressors (Meyer 2003). On top of this, we often live through vicarious trauma (Pearlman and MacIan 1995), such as hearing on the news that another Black trans woman has been murdered or learning from trans friends that they have been going through similar traumas to ourselves. This leads to proximal stressors (Meyer 2003), our internal processes that occur after external stress, such as fear of rejection, internalized transphobia, and shame.

These types of trauma come together to form a particular kind of trauma called minority stress (Meyer 2003). This is the trauma that comes with living as an oppressed person in a hostile and prejudiced society, as trans and/or non-binary people do. This experience leads to high stress, expectations of relational pain, having to live incongruently to avoid violence, internalized prejudice, and unhelpful coping mechanisms, such as substance abuse (Meyer 2003). It's been known for a long time that minority stress, plus the trauma and difficult social situations that come with it, hits hard in all areas of mental health (Dohrenwend 1966; Dohrenwend 2000) and can even affect our physical health (Pérez et al. 2012).

So, chances are you've experienced trauma in your life, and it stands to reason that you're in some way traumatized. This may or may not be new information to you – either way, pause for a moment and take a deep breath. This can be a very painful thing to think about and it's okay to feel that pain however it manifests for you. This pain, and this minority stress, means that you're more likely to need mental wellness practices that are geared toward helping you feel safe, connected, unashamed, and in control of your own life.

Shame and Internalized Oppression

Society would like us to believe that it is shameful to be trans (Al-Kadhi 2018). Even if we know this is not true, and believe that it is not true, we can still feel this shame about ourselves and others. Ideas like this can be introjected into our selves – that is, we all naturally absorb aspects of the world into our own belief systems, which can have positive, negative, and neutral effects (Rogers 1951; Feltham and Dryden 1993), including everything that might come with society's oppression of trans people. You don't pick up this shame on purpose, but rather you internalize it over time through societal attitudes, friends, family, media, and events where you've been made to feel ashamed, either personally or vicariously. This internalized transphobia can then inform your conditions of worth – that is, your inner experiences that inform your self-regard (Rogers 1951). In this way, societal transphobia can become *your* transphobia, influencing how you see yourself and how much you like and value yourself – and, if you feel strongly transphobic towards yourself, chances are you won't like or value yourself much at all. This level of shame can be a trauma in itself.

When you feel shame, what you're feeling is the sense that you are bad or wrong on a fundamental level. To combat this, it's important to learn that this is not true, and to learn this in such a way that you both know this intellectually and feel it emotionally. One of the ways to lessen this shame is to share how you're feeling with someone who offers empathy in return and can remind you that you are neither bad nor wrong (Brown 2013). Shame thrives when it is kept secret, so talking as openly as possible about your shame can help it to lessen.

While talking to others about your shame can be incredibly helpful, it's also worth examining how you talk to yourself, and treat yourself, when you feel shame. Is shame an emotion that you can hold, examine, and eventually let go, or is it a process that leaves you spiralling down into self-loathing? When you find yourself feeling ashamed of who you are or treating yourself as if you don't deserve care, take a deep breath and try to gently figure out what's happened. The shame you're experiencing is likely not your fault (which is definitely the case if you feel shame around being trans and/or non-binary), or if it is your fault, it's likely to be something you can learn and grow from. If you notice that you're talking to yourself with internalized oppression – for example, if you find yourself thinking that you're bad, gross, or intrinsically wrong – you can gently tell yourself that those thoughts aren't true and that they come from internalized oppression, so this is a belief that you can change. If you find yourself experiencing a lot of shame, take time often to remind yourself that everybody is human and nobody is perfect.

Something else that I do for myself a lot when I'm experiencing shame is to remind myself of the global truths I know about people and then deliberately apply them to myself. If I believe that human beings who are ashamed deserve compassion, and I recognize that I'm a human being, then I must deserve compassion. If I believe that trans people don't deserve to feel ashamed for who they are, and I recognize that I am trans, then I must not deserve to feel ashamed for who I am. Another similar tip is to take a little time to imagine a stranger who is going through the same life events and feelings as you and ask yourself what help and compassion you would offer that person – and then offer that to yourself.

It's also important to spend time being critical of the internal and external messages you pick up around how being trans is wrong, and to recognize that these messages are designed to bring you down and that they are not the truth. These messages will be coming at you from multiple sources, so try to pay attention to the people around you, the news you use, and the media you take in. However you feel is valid, and you might find yourself feeling a range of negative emotions, but try to point those emotions at the source and not at yourself. You don't deserve to feel ashamed – they do.

Fight, Flight, and Freeze

I've discussed how dealing with transphobic abuse, particularly as a non-passing or outed trans person, can be an extremely traumatic experience. Whether it's a stranger shouting a slur at you, bullies at your place of work, someone insisting you're in the 'wrong' toilet, or being aware that this happens in your community, the threat of danger can evoke a whole range of strong emotions, not just shame. Fear, anger, dread, anxiety, sadness, and numbness are common responses, sometimes all at the same time. It's okay to feel any of these things, or anything else, and feeling affected by abuse does not make you weak. There is no wrong way to be affected by abuse.

Trauma in these instances can, and probably will, invoke your 'fight' and 'flight' responses (Cannon 1932). This is what happens when your autonomic nervous system, the part of you that's in charge of responding to threats, triggers hormones and neurotransmitters, like adrenaline, that will prime your body and mind to escape danger. You enter a state of hyperarousal, your body's way of making you ready for action, and your focus will narrow on the dangerous event at hand. You usually do not get to decide whether or not to have this response, or whether you enter fight or flight mode.

When you enter a state of hyperarousal, this might involve

your body preparing to fight the abuse to make it stop. You may find yourself making aggressive eye contact, changing your body language to look bigger and tougher, or preparing to argue with or shout at your abusers. You might feel your arms becoming warm, your facial muscles tensing, your teeth gritting, your vision tunnelling, and your hands clenching into fists.

Alternatively, your body may prepare you for flight so you can quickly leave the abusive situation. You might find yourself avoiding eye contact, feeling your insides go cold and your leg muscles get warm, changing your body language so you look smaller, taking quicker steps, feeling increasingly aware of your surroundings, and looking for exits.

In either situation, you may find yourself breathing hard, shaking, and having a feeling of your body bracing itself for something bad to happen.

You may also find yourself 'freezing' so you're less noticeable during an abusive situation, a lesser known but equally strong response to traumatic events. You might find yourself having more difficulty moving, being less able to communicate in the ways you would usually find easy, feeling emotionally and/or physically numb, holding your breath, being unable to look away from the threat, and experiencing a wash of coldness over your body.

Your body will be going through these processes to protect you from trauma. They may seem unhelpful or feel confusing, but this is an ancient and important part of you that is trying to keep you safe (Cannon 1932). These coping mechanisms are especially likely to happen to you if you've faced trauma in the past. While sometimes fighting, fleeing, or freezing can be an extremely helpful reaction during traumatic situations, these coping mechanisms can sometimes pop up when they're not wanted. For example, you might find yourself freezing when you need to take action to be safe, fleeing from important conversations, or fighting with your partner over small issues. This may be happening because life has taught you to look out for threats all the time, and that small threats can escalate quickly into major traumas.

There are things you can do if you find yourself constantly responding in these ways, and they are mostly about reminding yourself that you are safe. Working to make your life as safe and relaxing as possible will bring your stress baseline down, meaning you may be less likely to respond to perceived threats in ways that aren't useful to you.

The Fawn Response

Along with the fight, flight, and freeze responses that are more commonly known, there is the fawn response (Walker 2003). This is a quick-acting, unintentional trauma response, like the other three Fs, that is designed to keep you safe in abusive situations, this time by 'fawning over' or playing up to the threat at hand, which is usually a person or institution. This is most likely to happen in people who have survived, or who are surviving, family and domestic abuse.

If you find yourself going through a fawn response, you will probably experience the most obvious signs of hyperarousal, such as breathing hard, shaking, and feeling 'braced' for something bad to happen. In this case, you'll also find yourself saying and doing things to defuse the threat in a gratifying and compliant manner, compulsively trying to please and soothe others while ignoring your own needs. You may find yourself feeling responsible for calming any traumatic situations, apologizing compulsively when you haven't done anything wrong, and suppressing your feelings or opinions so that other people don't become displeased with you. People may describe you as a 'people-pleaser', and when you were younger, people may have described you as 'mature for your age' because you were obedient and frightened of getting into trouble.

If you find yourself having fawn responses, remember that this is another way that your body is trying to keep you safe. When you've been in dangerous situations in the past where people have hurt you or threatened to hurt you, you will have learned that de-escalating the situation keeps you safe, so over time this will become a snap reaction that occurs when any threats are perceived. Much like the fight, flight, and freeze responses, you may find that any unwanted fawn responses are easier to divert when your general stress levels are lower and you feel safer in general. Distancing yourself from the original perpetrators of abuse, if you can, may also reduce your unintentional fawn response and keep you safe.

Feeling Safe

Steps to ensure your safety can be physical (such as finding suitable housing or making sure you're warm enough), relational (such as ending toxic relationships or saying hi to people who value you), cognitive (such as taking time out if you're feeling overwhelmed), and emotional (such as prioritizing activities and scenarios that make you feel safe). As a trans person living in a world that is often not safe, prioritizing all of these kinds of safety when you can is going to be so important for your well-being.

One act of self-care that applies to all of these safety situations is working on your boundaries. Take some time to have a serious think about what you need to feel safe right now and what you are prepared to do (or not prepared to do) to get there. It might help to write this as a chart or a list, with different types of safety (physical, relationships, thoughts, and feelings) listed as headings. Which of these kinds of safety need some work in your life? What could be improved, and how? Think outside the box and include things that don't feel quite possible right now – they're probably more doable than you think, if you can find a way to be flexible. Think about what changes you might have to say 'yes' to, what you're prepared to say 'maybe' to, and what you will need to say 'no' to in the future.

Counter-intuitively, making your daily life safe and comfortable can be really difficult and draining, so it's okay if you find yourself making small steps. It's also okay if the steps you're taking to be safe right now aren't always the most comfortable – like other aspects of self-care, sometimes being safe means snuggling in warm blankets and having a nice time with trusted friends, and other times it means making difficult decisions around work, family, and accommodation. Different types of safety will take priority at different times, and it won't always be fun but it will always make your life better in some way.

Safety Breathing

Something that I find works with many of my clients, and with myself if I'm feeling unsafe, is to do something I call safety breathing. This is a variation on box breathing, which is a type of breath work designed to make you feel less stressed (Farhi 1996).

Take a breath in for the count of four. At the top of the breath, pause to say out loud or in your head, 'I am safe.' Exhale for the count of four. At the bottom of the breath, pause again to repeat, 'I am safe.' Do this for as long as you like.

It can help to put a hand on your chest so you can feel your breath going in and out, if this doesn't give you dysphoria. The idea to breathe in and out for the count of four is also only a guide – you can breathe in and out for as long or as short a count as feels comfortable for you. The idea is to breathe in a controlled and equal manner, as this can help you to feel less anxious and more safe in your body. The verbal reminder that you're safe can also gently hammer the point home.

Chronic Stress and General Adaptation Syndrome

During traumatic events that lead to acute stress – the kinds that happen relatively suddenly and are over relatively quickly – you'll usually find yourself entering fight, flight, or freeze, and then 'coming down' from the shock over a short amount of time.

When the stress you experience is chronic – that is, when it happens over a long period of time with very little reprieve – there is no coming-down period. You continue to be stressed, in body and in mind, until the stressful experience stops. Unfortunately, it's often very stressful to be trans due to internal (e.g. dysphoria), distal (e.g. discrimination), and proximal (e.g. internalized transphobia) stressors (Meyer 2003), so you might find yourself experiencing stress chronically.

After a long period of chronic stress, your body starts to get used to this state of being and adapts, as best it can, to what it perceives as a lifetime of stress. If you can't resist or escape the source of trauma, your body will do its best to get used to it. This can lead to General Adaptation Syndrome (Selye 1950), a physical, cognitive, and emotional reaction to stressful events.

General Adaptation Syndrome is something that happens over a long period of time. After the initial shock or alarm of a traumatic event – usually accompanied by a fight, flight, freeze, or fawn reaction – your body's initial response is to stay alert but to try to repair itself by reducing blood pressure, levelling out hormone levels, and balancing breathing back to your usual levels. If you don't have the chance to recover from the stressful event or events, your body won't be able to balance out and you may struggle to come out of your state of alertness as your body resists what is happening. Your body will try to adapt to this as best it can but, over time, you'll begin to feel exhausted as your body tries to stay alert (Fink 2016).

All of this means your concentration will be affected, your mood might be low or erratic, you might struggle to sleep, and you might feel easily stressed or upset. You might find yourself in fight, flight, freeze, or fawn states that don't match up with current events. You may feel startled when nothing happens, irritable out of nowhere, or suddenly tearful without knowing why. Over time, you might develop anxiety, burnout, or depression. This level of ongoing stress can also affect your immune system and you might be more at risk of illness.

A way to combat this is to try to complete the trauma cycle as soon as you can after something bad happens to you. Take the time you need after something difficult has happened to you and engage in the best self-care you can as soon as you can. Specifically focusing on self-care that helps you feel safe, calm, physically rested, and grounded in your body can help you to reach the state of balance that stops stress from becoming chronic. There are some great ideas in the *Self-Care* chapter of this book.

Something else that I've found helpful for clients is spending time tackling the smaller stresses in your life, even if you can't do much about the bigger ones right now. This might look like very consciously making small but important choices in your life, making sure you complete them, and then deliberately observing this ending. That might look like finishing something on your to-do list or completing a fun task that you started a while ago but never got round to winding up, and then doing something nice for yourself afterwards to celebrate. This gives your mind and your body a chance to recalibrate to the recovery stage of stress, hopefully bringing your overall stress levels down.

Physically and emotionally resting is also a good idea, as you are likely to feel exhausted in multiple ways. If you feel that you have to take more breaks than other people, remember that it's okay to need rest and that your body is going through an intense physical reaction that you are still recovering from. It's okay to rest when you're ill (and in general)!

Isolation Is Traumatic

As a trans person, you're likely to be facing some kind of social exclusion due to society's transphobia. Being excluded by society influences your sense of trust (Hillebrandt, Sebastian, and Blakemore 2011) and, without a stable and welcoming place in society, you may start to question who you are. Isolation can be very painful, and social exclusion and oppression are even processed by the body in the same way as physical pain (Pieritz et al. 2017; Canaipa et al. 2016).

One of the ways I've seen clients, especially trans women, try to deal with this is by further isolating themselves, which decreases the risk of distal traumas like being attacked, but increases proximal traumas by magnifying shame, lowering self-esteem, and decreasing the resources available to them.

One of the best ways to fight the trauma of isolation is to find your community and strengthen your social threads. Social support and quality relationships can have profound impacts on our mental well-being, and one of the best ways we can heal from trauma is through relationship (Hope 2019). Your personal community involves anyone who you feel connected to and who can offer you support. This might include family, chosen family, friends, colleagues, partners, support groups, professionals working with and for you, and anyone who you feel comfortable with. Your social threads may feel particularly strong with other trans and/or non-binary people, as they are least likely to see you through an oppressive lens. Your chosen community can also include your wider community, and a connection to your local and global LGBTQ+ community can be very important for your well-being (Hendricks and Testa 2012).

If finding community is too difficult to do in person, there are so many ways to find like-minded people online, and these online possibilities are only increasing over time. There are many ways to find friendship and community if it does not feel safe to meet people in conventional ways. If you like video games, there are also several Twitch streams run by trans streamers who ensure a comfortable, calm, and LGBTQ+-friendly community while they stream video games for others to watch and, sometimes, participate in (a personal favourite as of 2021 is Stef Sanjati's stream,* which prioritizes cosiness and inclusivity). There are also many welcoming groups online in places like Facebook and Discord, while you can find kind people who enjoy the same hobbies as you in places like Twitter and Instagram. There are some resources for some online communities you can join in the *Charities, Helplines, and Other Free Advice* chapter of this book.

* www.twitch.tv/thestefsanjati/about

As an aside, if you find yourself staying in for the majority of your time, it may be worth taking vitamin D supplements. A deficiency of vitamin D, which your body produces when you're out in the sun, can negatively affect your mood. You can visit your doctor for a blood test to see if you have a deficiency or, if this isn't possible for you, you can find basic vitamin D supplements in supermarkets or health shops in store and online.

Dealing with Transphobic Abuse Online

The internet has made it possible for trans and/or non-binary people of all kinds, from all over the world, to meet and share support. Unfortunately, this is also true of transphobes, who use the internet to connect, organize, bully, and troll, all of which can be very traumatic for trans people (Compton 2019). This is traumatic not just for the individual trans person being abused, but also for any trans person watching the abuse happen.

The emotionally abusive tactics of individual transphobes and 'gender-critical' organizations are often reminiscent of those of domestic abusers (Snow 2021a). They will harass and dehumanize their targets while charming others, co-opting bystanders to assist with the abuse, and labelling the abused as 'crazy' and unreliable (Herman 1992). In both cases, the powerful perpetrators try to keep their targets downtrodden and anyone else either quiet or complicit (Hope 2019), while loudly stating that the abuse survivor is lying, exaggerating, delusional, or asking for it (Herman 1992). This level of sustained abuse is also reminiscent of conversion therapy, a specific type of abuse that utilizes endless emotional harassment, criticism, humiliation, and gaslighting to try to change an integral part of someone that others see as abhorrent (Snow 2021a; Schevers 2021b). This level of abuse is especially easy to implement online as the internet is so far-reaching with few boundaries, particularly on social media and on platforms where abusers can be anonymous.

Try to remember that there's no wrong way to deal with bullying and abuse. Abusers will try to make you feel wrong no matter what your approach, so try to go with what you need instead of what you think is the 'right' response. If you choose to respond to online abuse, it might be worth taking a minute to ask yourself why you want to say what you want to say. Who does it benefit? Will it genuinely help you, the person you're responding to, or anyone else? Even if it helps someone else, will it take anything away from you?

Responding to trolls online can also be a relatively subtle form of self-harm. When things feel hopeless, when you are angry at the injustice in the world, or when your self-esteem is low, you may find yourself searching on social media for transphobic messages with the intent to respond, to block, or to keep up to date with the messages transphobes are spreading. There is good intent behind this, but taking in these messages is likely to increase your feelings of hopelessness and anger, and to further lower your self-esteem. My advice is to react however you feel is appropriate to any abuse that you come across but not to go looking for it.

Even if you're not searching for abusers, you may find that they come to you. Remember that the feelings of these abusers are about themselves and how they see the world – they are not true to who you are. Your fight, flight, freeze, or fawn response might kick in, just like if someone was abusing you to your face; it's okay to take your time to calm down, look after yourself, and decide what you would like to do. Respond, or don't respond, in a way that you think will benefit you. Remember that there is no shame in blocking abusers, muting them, unfollowing them, or locking down your social media accounts; this is not a game that you can lose and it's healthy to put boundaries around who can interact with you. It may also be a good idea to report any abuse that comes your way to increase the chances that they won't come back.

After you've received online abuse, you may also want to take a minute to check in with yourself and give yourself what you need after the experience, whether this is something to help you feel safe, a way to healthily let out your anger, or seeking support from someone you trust.

Dealing with Transphobic Abuse in the Media

Just because abuse isn't aimed at you personally, doesn't mean it's not abuse. Your body and brain will likely process a threat to trans people as a threat aimed at you (which, in many ways, it is), leading to vicarious and personal trauma. Much like the abusive trolling that happens on social media, the wider media can be seen to engage in abuse tactics and microaggressions against the trans community as a whole (Compton 2019; Snow 2021b). People and organizations can and will use the media to undermine, devalue, and actively hurt trans people, using the news and other publications to attempt to rollback our rights.

Sometimes, it can help to remember that these companies knowingly write lies about us, and who you really are is never reflected in transphobic articles. If this doesn't help and this media only makes you angry, that's okay, too – anger is a signal that something is wrong and unfair, and we can use that energy to make the changes we need to make, like campaigning for justice and engaging in mutual aid. If seeing transphobic media just makes you feel exhausted, take the opportunity to rest and take care of yourself, or to connect with your community – the very things that this kind of media wants to deny you. There's power in however you're feeling in reaction to transphobic media and you can harness that to care for yourself and others.

It's also worth sticking to news sources that you know are less likely to be transphobic but are still well informed, like PinkNews and the What the Trans!? podcast. Even when the media addresses trans issues respectfully, bad news for the trans community can still be incredibly traumatic, so it's okay to limit the amount of news you consume in a day. There can be a fine line to tread between staying informed and hurting yourself. It's okay to take a break from engaging with the news if it feels like it's becoming too much. Whatever 'too much' looks like will be up to you and how you feel.

And, as always, don't read the comments (Hunte 2019).

Dealing Well with 'Small t' Family Trauma

All families have some minor difficulties, and some of these difficulties may be around your gender identity. For example, your family might be generally accepting of your gender but they might consistently struggle with your pronouns, or they may show you lots of love and support but not seem to understand what being transgender actually means. Even though these difficult situations might not seem too bad in the grand scheme of things, they can still be quite painful, especially when these instances build up over time.

In circumstances where your family is supportive in some areas but not in others, it can be really useful to learn how to be assertive. This should ensure people take notice of your needs while avoiding hurt on either side. Try to use 'I' statements in a neutral voice, at a respectful distance, with relaxed body language and non-aggressive eye contact. An example of a neutral, simple, assertive, and non-hurtful statement might be, 'I use they/them pronouns and I need you to use them when you refer to me.' This level of assertiveness might be difficult in the moment but it increases your chances of being heard, which increases the chances of your loved ones respecting your wishes now and in the future. If the other person or people try to argue back to you: show them that you've heard them (which is not to say you've agreed with what they've said); say what you think or feel; and say what you need to happen. For example, the statement might sound something like this: 'I hear that you think you might not be able to remember my correct pronouns all the time. I understand that this might be a hard change for you, but I feel sad when you misgender me and happy when you use my correct pronouns. I need you to keep trying to use my pronouns.' Showing you've heard someone can bring you both to the same level, as well as unbalance them if they were prepared to go on the offensive or defensive; saying how you feel shows what you have to say matters, too, while using 'I' statements shows you own your feelings in a non-apologetic way; and saying what you need to happen might bring about results.

Dealing Well with 'Big T' Family Trauma

People who are supposed to support you can be really horrible about your gender, sometimes in ways that really damage you. Sometimes, this means extreme events occur that make you feel unloved, unwanted, and unsafe around the people who said they would always protect you. For example, maybe you tried to come out to your family and they were verbally abusive, or maybe they found your secret clothes that make you feel gender euphoria and they were physically violent towards you. It can be so much worse when these people are your family, because it can feel like you're stuck with them for the rest of your life, trapped between a rock and a hard place. You don't have to take this from them just because you love them. There are ways to deal with this without putting up and shutting up.

If there's anybody that you trust outside of your family, open up to them about what has happened. Let someone know that an event has occurred that made you unsafe and talk about how you're feeling. If you need help, think about how you can ask for it and how you feel best receiving it. If you know anyone who can offer you practical support, like making sure you have enough to eat or giving you a physical space to keep important things, it's okay to ask for it. What would make you safe right now?

Have a think about what you might need going forwards to feel safe again. Can you be around your family right now, or do you need to find somewhere else to be for a while? Do you feel okay to be around your family (or maybe it's practically impossible to leave) but you need to interact with them in a very boundaried way? Can you safely talk with your family about what happened or do you need space?

Dealing well with this kind of trauma is all about getting what you need to feel safe and heal from the traumatic event. It's important that you do everything you can to keep yourself safe and that you put yourself first.

Transphobic Red Flags in Relationships

A 'red flag' is a sign that a relationship may be toxic, abusive, dangerous, or otherwise not good for you. Red flags can come up in all kinds of relationships – romantic, sexual, platonic, familial, etc. They can be direct, like when someone is rude to serving staff at a restaurant (flagging up that they tend to be rude in general, even if they haven't shown that to you yet), or more subtle, like when you feel especially drained after the person leaves (flagging up that they might be taking more than you can give right now).

An example of a red flag in all relationships is when the other person uses your chosen name and pronouns to your face but refuses to use them around other people because they feel embarrassed, ashamed, or like they don't need to try if you can't hear. Please note that this is not the same as when someone has your permission to use different pronouns or a deadname in order to protect you from harm or to not out you when you are still in the closet in certain situations. The flag becomes a red one when this happens without your consent or consideration, and it's often a sign of disrespect.

When you spot a red flag, or generally notice aspects of your relationships that make you feel uncomfortable or on edge, take a moment to think about how you feel. What exactly are your emotions and what are they telling you? If you're confused, is it because this person is disorienting you? If you're angry, is it because something about the relationship has become unfair? Think about your needs and your boundaries – are you getting your needs met while this behaviour happens, and how much are your boundaries being crossed by this action?

If you can, talk to the other person about your feelings and what's been going on for you. Explain that their behaviour is a red flag and that, for both of you, you want to nip it in the bud to stop it from becoming a deal-breaker. Tell them what you'll need from them and listen carefully to their response. In a healthy relationship, the person who hoisted the red flag will listen to you, clarify what you need without becoming defensive (or they will at least recognize if they have become defensive and correct this), and work on this behaviour. For example, if you tell someone that you're very uncomfortable with them using your deadname and the wrong pronouns when they speak about you, the person should listen to you, make sure they understand the situation properly, and make sure to use your real name and pronouns in conversations from then on.

While one or two red flags here or there might just be a sign that you need to talk and work something out, it's worth looking at what makes you feel uncomfortable or unsafe in your relationships and figuring out your boundaries and deal-breakers so that you know when to talk to someone and when to cut your losses. It's okay to trust your intuition about whether you're safe in a relationship.

A Short Course in Getting What You Need in a Disagreement

DEAR MAN is a series of mini skills, taught in Dialectical Behavioural Therapy (DBT) (Linehan 2015; Brantley, Wood, and McKay 2007), that make up one big skill – assertive and non-damaging conflict resolution (Spradlin 2003; Linehan 2015). It's designed to help people who aren't good at asking for help make requests without hurting themselves or their relationships.

Even if you're not outright asking for something, the skills can come in handy when you're gearing up for a hard conversation, or they can help you to stay calm and say 'no' when you're asked to do something you don't want to.

For some people, standing up for their wants can be really scary. For others, it's difficult to keep a cool head when another person is pushing their boundaries. Even so, I always think it's worth trying to resolve non-abusive conflicts with nobody getting hurt, if you can. Maybe DEAR MAN can help you make that happen.

- *D is for Describe.* When you're asking for something or fighting your corner in a conflict, start by describing the facts of your situation. If you state facts about what's going on for you, as opposed to opinions, the other person can't disagree with you, and you're already one step ahead of an escalation.

- *E is for Express.* You've just set up the facts of your situation. Now is the time to talk about how the facts make you feel, and to state your personal interpretation of those facts. Use statements that start with 'I' and centre yourself, e.g. 'I think' and 'I feel', because if you're talking about how you feel and not what someone else has done, it's more difficult for them to get defensive. Try your best not to be rude or hurtful – nothing will make someone switch off to your requests faster – but don't budge on genuinely expressing how you feel.

- *The first A is for Assert.* The facts are lined up and your perspective, thoughts, and feelings are backing them up. Now it's time to assert what you want and need. Be as clear and direct as possible. This can be really scary and difficult, especially if you're nervous or emotions are generally running high, but it's necessary if you want to be properly understood. Try not to use hedging phrases like 'maybe', 'a bit', or 'I guess' – they can be really hard to shake off, but this will help you sound clearer in what you want.

- *R is for Reinforce.* When you're making a request or laying down a boundary, it's important to reinforce that this is a positive thing. Remind the person that what you're asking for, and even the fact that you're asking, is a healthy thing – this is going to make your life better, and your relationship stronger.

- *M is for Mindfulness.* It's not just a buzzword, I promise! Mindfulness here means focusing on your desired outcome and the issue at hand. Try not to get distracted by anything else, like going off on a tangent or adding 'And another thing'. Try not to get caught up in worrying about the future and try not to make any promises you don't want to make. It's also not the time for fighting about the past – it really won't help.

- *The second A is for Appearances.* Try your best to look like you believe in what you're saying. Confidence, calmness, and openness are all important stances to try to embody. I know that when I'm in a conflict or asking for something difficult, I tend to look embarrassed, making me look like I've already lost. It's a difficult habit to shake but the more confident you look, the more the other person knows how seriously you take this and how much you believe you deserve what you want (and you do deserve it!). Keep reminding yourself to sit tall, relax your shoulders, and make pleasant eye contact, if you can. If you struggle to make eye contact, it can help to look at someone's eyebrows or the bridge of their nose instead.

- *N is for Negotiate.* You can't always get exactly what you need, and you can't always win 100% of every argument.

That's okay, because a situation where you both win is best for your relationship, even if your own win is only 90%. If the other person can't give you what you ask for, it's okay to look again at what you need and ask if you can get that a different way that will help everybody feel like they've won.

Cutting Ties with Transphobic and Abusive Relationships

Sometimes, people can hurt you so much that you need, or want, to walk away.

It's okay; it's not your fault. You have to put your own safety first, whether physical or psychological. You deserve respect. You deserve to express yourself and your interests without restrictions on who you should be, set by people who are supposed to care for you no matter what. That kind of conditional love can be dangerous, and it is not your responsibility to respect people who are cruel to you. It is not your fault if other people have been intolerable to you.

I repeat – *it is not your fault.*

Cutting ties can take many forms, depending on your individual situation. Sometimes, it means sitting down with the other person and telling them why this is happening before you go; sometimes, it's sending a message before blocking them; sometimes, it's packing your things while they're out and going somewhere safe. You need to think about what's best, and what's safest, for you.

Walking away is going to hurt. It may well turn your life upside down. Be as ready as you can be, go as safely as you can go, get your support network on your side, be as emotional as you need to about it, and try to do things that make you feel happy and strong, even if it's just taking a few hours a week to do something calm or fun that's just for you. Explain to everyone you can what's going on. Remember that looking after yourself is not an indulgence but a necessity, and keep being the awesome you that you know you are.

Getting Through the Trauma of Coming Out (Again and Again)

The media tends to show coming out as a big, life-changing, one-time event, after which we've officially Come Out. This is rarely true in real life, and we often find ourselves coming out multiple times. This could be for many reasons, for example because you have lots of friends you need to come out to, because you need to correct people's pronouns often, or because your paperwork shows a different gender to the one you are. For some, especially those who work in customer-facing jobs, this could mean coming out every day.

Coming out can be a joyful experience of connection between people, and it can also be a really unpleasant necessity. Trans people tend to be particularly vulnerable when they are just starting to come out (Hope 2019), and starting to come out to important people in your life can be nerve-wracking even if you're certain that they'll be supportive, never mind when you think they may not understand or when you think they may have a negative reaction. When you find yourself coming out to people often, this usually involves being initially misgendered and can be both painful and very draining. It's also difficult to know how strangers will react to you coming out, and this uncertainty can be a scary experience. The knowledge that this could happen often in your life can leave you feeling anxious, frustrated, or hopeless.

When you find yourself coming out to important people in your life, it's likely that this is something you'll have thought about and that you want to prepare in advance. Try to keep your safety and comfort in mind when you plan what, where, and how you will tell people. For example, if you're telling your boss that you want to change your name on the work system because you are trans, you will likely have different needs to consider than if you're telling your long-term partner. To reduce the likelihood of experiencing harm or a breakdown of communication from the people or person you're coming out to, it can be helpful to consider what specific information and emotions you need to get across to them and have more in-depth resources available to share if more questions are asked. This can give everybody involved the time and space to process what has happened with minimal communication breakdown.

An example might look like this. If you're planning to come out to your mum, who you know loves and supports you but has said in the past that she doesn't 'get this whole trans thing', you might consider coming out to her somewhere you can both feel relaxed but where you can quickly set a hard boundary, for example over the phone (which allows you to hang up) or at a familiar cafe (that you know you can leave easily). You might want someone else you trust there with you, or you might just want to see your mum on your own, depending on how you feel. You might want to plan the information you need to convey in advance and to just say what you need for now, for example 'Mum, I've known for some time now that I'm non-binary. For me, that means I'm not a boy or a girl. I need you to use they/them pronouns for me, and to use my chosen name from now on. I love you.' If your mum then asks for further information, you can either answer if you feel safe or have some resources ready to go, for example websites, books, or YouTube videos. Know that any negative or traumatic events that might follow are never your fault and are never deserved.

When you find yourself coming out to strangers, it's worth holding on to the knowledge that how others see you is rarely about who you actually are and much more about how they process the world. If they misgender you, it is because they are seeing you through an internal lens based in cissexism and binarism, and who you are is much more than they can see. Correcting people and coming out to them can have many different responses, from the negative, to the neutral, to the positive, and there's no wrong way to process any of these outcomes. Allow yourself the space and time to process any thoughts and feelings you have after coming out. It can also help to have people on hand that you know will validate you when people have invalidated your identity.

It's also okay if you don't come out to everyone, or at all. Coming out should always be about your safety, your comfort, your joy, and your choice. There's no shame in staying in the closet sometimes, or all the time, and this doesn't make you any less trans.

When Past Trauma Makes Itself Present

In my experience as a therapist, unresolved trauma rarely stays in the past. You might find yourself reliving your worst moments in multiple ways; nightmares, intrusive thoughts about events, involuntary memories, and emotional flashbacks can all be common ways for your brain to try to keep you safe and process what happened (van der Hart, Bolt, and van der Kolk 2005; Hirsch and Holmes 2007).

It can feel like your brain is making you relive your worst times to punish you, but this is not true. These thoughts, feelings, memories, and images are probably coming up for you because you are still trying to process and make peace with what has happened to you, and because your brain is still trying to process this past information to make your present and future more safe (Herman 1992; van der Kolk 1994; van der Kolk and Fisler 1995; Hopper *et al.* 2007). One of your brain's main jobs is to keep you safe and it works really hard at this, even when it feels really painful.

You might also find yourself experiencing emotional flashbacks. This is when you experience an emotion that is rooted in your past experience of trauma and not fully in the present moment. This might be something that's very obvious to you, for example when you suddenly feel explosive anger out of what feels like nowhere or when you find yourself suddenly sobbing during a quiet moment. Sometimes, however, emotional flashbacks can be very subtle, and you may not know exactly if what you're feeling belongs to the present or the past. After some practice of being very aware of how you're doing, it should also get easier to spot more subtle examples in your life. It can be helpful to check in with how you're thinking and feeling with these questions.

- Do your thoughts align with your emotions? (E.g. if someone makes a surprising noise and you think the words, 'Please don't hurt me,' or if you feel angry because you broke a plate and you think the words, 'Leave me alone!', you might be having an emotional flashback.)

- Where is your emotion present in your body? (E.g. if you usually feel anxiety in your chest but a present event or person makes you feel anxiety in your throat, was there another time or person that made you feel that way?)

- Do your thoughts or feelings have a different 'flavour' than usual? (E.g. you might find yourself feeling or thinking in a way that is 'younger' than usual or saying things that remind you of words someone else has said to you.)

- Does your activated behaviour match the event? (E.g. you might find yourself flinching like you've been hit if someone uses a specific tone of voice or blurting out an apology for seemingly no reason.)

- If you find yourself having nightmares, intrusive thoughts, flashbacks, and/or intrusive images, try to keep in mind that your memories are running in the background and you are learning new ways to integrate this information in a safe way. Pushing away these thoughts and images can just make them keep popping up later. It can be very helpful to stop what you're doing for a moment if it's safe to do so, take some really deep breaths to steady yourself, and remind yourself strongly that you are currently safe. It can be useful to think hard about what's different right now compared to when the traumatic events happened; think about who you are, where you are, the different time you're in, who you're with, the different things you know. Look around you and connect to the space you're in by noticing what you can see, feel, hear, smell, and taste. Chances are, you're in a safer place in at least some small ways than you were then. Remind yourself as much as you can that you are now safer than you were when the traumatic event happened.

Community Support

Whoever you've been excluded by in the past, finding supportive and inclusive people in your current life can help to put this trauma to rest and increase your feelings of belonging, sense of control, self-esteem, positive emotions, and purpose (Tang and Richardson 2013).

Mutual aid is important when you've faced trauma (Seebohm *et al.* 2013). If you can give what you can and take what you need, this can increase your sense of physical and emotional safety by reminding you that others can care for you and that you're capable of caring for others (Buczynski and Porges 2012). Co-regulating your emotions with others – which here means experiencing emotions with others, offering mutual reassurance, and reaching a stable emotional level together – can help you to feel connected to others and to yourself (Dana 2020). This support can come from friends, family, your local community, online support networks, and your care team. When you're cared about in a reliable and continuous way, this predictability can help you to feel fully at ease and part of the wider world (Baumeister and Leary 1995). Community support, mutual aid, and mutual advocating can be particularly important and effective with other queer, transgender, and non-binary people (Jackson Levin *et al.* 2020). After living with trauma, being together with people who understand a vital part of your identity and experience can be a healing, comforting, and energizing experience.

Protesting as Safety (Safely)

In most of the world, including the UK, passively and actively transphobic laws can make us feel really unsafe in a way that permeates all corners of our lives. Protesting these laws, individually and as part of your community, can help you feel more powerful in the face of this traumatic injustice, while hopefully securing a practically safer future.

Different ways of standing up for yourself may make you feel more or less safe. Emailing your MP, calling elected officials, or signing an online petition, for example, can be excellent ways to advocate for your needs without the risk of being physically hurt.

You may also feel called to attend protests in person, increasing your impact and sense of power but possibly putting yourself at risk of violence. If you decide to attend a protest, it's important to keep yourself as physically and psychologically safe as you can. Remember to take water and snacks, and try to make sure nothing about you (like your hair or clothes) can be easily grabbed. Make sure your clothing and shoes are comfortable, waterproof, and indistinct, and that any of your distinctive features (like tattoos and piercings) are covered. Go with people you trust if you can, and take an old phone with important numbers ready to call. You might also want to bring a notepad, a pen, earplugs, wet wipes, and some basic first aid supplies. Leave any valuables or sentimental items at home so they don't get damaged or lost. Make sure that you're able to get away quickly if any trouble occurs (your safety is the most important thing).

If you'd like to know more about how to stay safe as a trans person if you are arrested at a protest, the organization Green and Black Cross has some excellent and inclusive information on this (Green and Black Cross 2017). Much of this information has also come from Liberty, which fights for human rights in the UK (Liberty 2021).

Only you will know what feels safest for you, and it's okay to put your safety first here. Anything that you can do for your community will be enough and hurting yourself for the good of others actually doesn't do that much good. Sometimes, the best way that we can protest unjust treatment is just to stay safe and alive.

Finding Power in Your Gender

Trauma is so often about the pain we feel when we are made helpless and powerless (Herman 1992). Doing things that make you feel powerful, or like you have some control over your life, can be a great way to counteract the effects of trauma.

Luckily, you're already stronger and more in control than you probably think you are, just by being yourself! Being trans is so powerful (Roche 2019) – you get to make so many choices about who you are and where you want to end up. You are in control of so much more than this world wants you to believe, and you can manifest your own destiny with your voice, clothes, hair, words, medication, and so much more. You have the power to reconstruct yourself from the inside out and the outside in – and you have the power to choose not to, to change and grow in other ways, to be yourself in any ways you want.

As hard as being trans can be, there's a kind of creative magic to it that's a real gift. You might find it useful to take some time, in your journal or in your head, to think about your gender and your transition so far and to think about which parts make you feel powerful or in control. What decisions have you made that have helped you to feel in charge of your body? What have you changed about yourself that has helped you to live the life you've always wanted? In what ways have you taken back control of your life in the wake of trauma, difficulty, or discomfort? You will have made these changes before and you will make these changes again. You are so powerful just by being you!

Trauma-Related Growth

In the aftermath of trauma, you might find that something about you or your life has changed for the better. It's also worth considering that a big effect that traumatic experiences can have is to make you feel like you've been stripped of your agency or like you never had any to begin with.

Taking steps towards making positive changes for you and your community is a great way to combat the effects of trauma while also working towards self-actualization. Trauma is often a catalyst for great amounts of change in many areas of your life, and some of this change may be good. Healing after trauma can facilitate self-discovery, learning from new experiences, and an active view towards self-management of well-being and self-care (Slade *et al.* 2019), all of which are amazing changes that you can concentrate on if you can. Remember that, when life gives you lemons, you don't have to make lemonade – you can make anything that tastes good to you. There's no pressure for you to have grown or to feel good after any amount of trauma, but know that you can affect your own destiny and take direct action to make your life better than it is now. You can make a change – not just that, but you can change for the better.

Depression

In this chapter, we'll explore issues like what depression might look and feel like to you, the ways in which dysphoria and social stigma can make us feel depressed, how to increase your self-esteem and emotional energy, and how to stop life from seeming hopeless (because, I promise, there's hope).

What Is Depression?

Depression is the experience of having low mood, diminished interest or pleasure in daily life, a slowing down of thought processes, physical fatigue, a loss of emotional and cognitive energy, low concentration, and executive dysfunction. This often comes with feelings of worthlessness, hopelessness, and guilt (American Psychiatric Association 2013).

Depression can look and feel like so many things, but what most therapy clients I've known who have been diagnosed with depression describe is a crushing sense of numbness, the kind of heavy, exhausting, physically painful sadness that makes you feel like nothing of who you are is left any more. The strong feelings you experience during depression can also include anger, irritability, coldness, anxiety, dread, and hopelessness – or you may feel like you've stopped having any emotions at all. You will probably experience low motivation, a lack of executive function (your 'get up and go'), getting too much or too little sleep, no appetite, pessimism and cynicism about the future, difficulty doing the things you used to enjoy, and very low self-esteem. I remember describing the feeling to a therapist as it being like something had pulped out all of who I was before, leaving only the very worst of me behind.

More than half of trans people have reported being diagnosed with depression at some point in their lives (FRA 2012) with as many as 88% showing symptoms of depression (McNeil *et al.* 2012). While being transgender can be joyful to neutral in many ways, it can also be pretty depressing, especially as we experience high rates of depressing life events like family rejection, bullying, lack of societal acceptance, and gender dysphoria (Johnson *et al.* 2019). Trans people also tend to have lower self-esteem and higher rates of interpersonal problems because of these difficulties, which are proximal traits that tend to go hand in hand with depression (Witcomb *et al.* 2018).

Are You Depressed?

It can be difficult to know whether you're depressed or not, which can be a surprising thing to hear given how strongly I've just described the experience. I think this is because depression can come on slowly over time, particularly when people have been fighting through traumatic circumstances for a while. As noted in the *Trauma* chapter of this book, you are much more likely to have experienced long-term stress and sadness than you might realize. As such, if you have been trying to work through an influx of traumatic events in your life, and are becoming steadily more tired and sad, it can be easy to slip into a state of depression without really realizing it. I, and many of my therapy clients, have experienced that cold and dreadful feeling of looking at your life and realizing that things are much worse than you realized.

If you're not sure if you're experiencing depression, take a look at your actions, your circumstances, and the way you think about yourself. Try to put aside thoughts of what is 'normal', how you 'should' feel, or whether anyone else has it 'worse' than you. This is 100% about you, if only for a little while. Do you find yourself feeling disconnected from the things you used to enjoy, without finding new things to fill their place? Have you noticed yourself feeling emotionally and physically tired in a way you didn't before, to the point that it influences your life? Do you think you're unworthy of good things, things that you think everyone else is worthy of? Have you found yourself thinking that life would be better if you weren't in it, or that things would be better if everything would just stop?

It may also help to ask any trusted friends, family, or members of your care team (like doctors, therapists, social workers, and community practitioner nurses) how you've been behaving lately. Ask them if you've seemed low, down, or low energy lately. Depression might look to others like you don't have any emotional or physical energy or that all you seem to show lately is sadness and a sense of worthlessness with no room for anything else, no matter how much they try to cheer you up. It might seem like you're smiling and on the go all the time lately, like you're trying to avoid something. It might seem like you're acting recklessly, talking about how you might as well not be here or not taking care of yourself in the ways you usually would.

Of course, you might also just look and act like you always have to everyone else, but inside it feels like everything is collapsing and everything feels much more difficult than it used to.

Dysphoria and Mood

If you have dysphoria, you probably don't need to be told that it can be really depressing. Trans people who experience dysphoria show higher rates of anxiety and depression than cis people (Dhejne *et al.* 2016).

It's no wonder that dysphoria is depressing. Although dysphoria can be most keenly felt about certain parts of your body, it can affect every part of your life, including your self-esteem, your hopefulness for the future, and how isolated you feel. It can make you not want to use your voice, physically and metaphorically, and it can make you feel uncomfortable and 'wrong' on many levels. In this way, dysphoria can greatly increase feelings of hopelessness, despair, sadness, and exhaustion that can fuel depression.

A piece of good news is that levels of depression influenced by dysphoria often drop significantly to 'control'/average levels after receiving gender-affirmative health care (Dhejne *et al.* 2016). It also stands to reason that any changes you can make that positively affect your dysphoria can help to lift your mood. When you're feeling depressed it can be incredibly difficult to work towards your gender transition, but any small change you can make for yourself will help. This might look like independent voice training (speaking out loud to see if you can speak higher or lower, depending on what feels best), turning your mirrors around and covering the back with fun stickers, shaving or letting your body hair grow, talking with other trans people, pampering the parts of your body that you do like, and much more.

As always, it's also a good idea to fully embrace whatever gives you a sense of gender euphoria. It can be excellent self-care to explore your sense of gender euphoria, and this can be particularly helpful when you're feeling depressed. Using prosthetics and aids that make you feel at home in your body, such as packers and breast forms, can help to alleviate your dysphoria and depression. So can self-care activities that make you feel connected to your euphoria, like styling your hair or wearing your favourite outfit.

Learned Helplessness at the Start of Your Transition

Learned helplessness is the theory that if you often experience traumas that you can't escape from, you will stop trying to escape from further trauma (Seligman, Maier, and Solomon 1971; Vollmayr and Gass 2013) – because what's the point, if you've learned that you're likely trapped in the situation forever? This hopelessness can pervade even if you know that it is irrational – for example, you may know that your wait for reconstructive gender surgery will one day be over, but your past experiences of trauma may also have you feeling that the day will never come. The belief that this is uncontrollable and uncertain can weigh you down surprisingly quickly (Firth and Brewin 1982). Facets of dysphoria, experiences of transphobia, and having to wait for your necessary aspects of transition can lead to you feeling trapped and helpless, which can, in turn, lead to depression (Nolen-Hoeksema, Girgus, and Seligman 1986; Maiden 1987).

Learned helplessness can lead to behaviours that can both

make you depressed and rob you of your ability to change your circumstances for the better. You're also likely to experience executive dysfunction, where you experience a loss of your energy and ability to plan, solve problems, organize your life, and manage your time. For example, you might find yourself procrastinating on getting important things done because you're worried you'll do them wrong, or you might experience a huge sadness and loss of energy when you run into a problem you know you could have solved easily in the past.

The good news is that this feeling is likely to lessen as you start to make changes in your life and in your transition (Costa and Colizzi 2016; Wang and Delgado 2021). The more you learn that change can happen and that things can get better, the less helpless you'll feel. It's worth pushing yourself a little to make some small decisions or changes (like redecorating your work space, deciding on an activity for the weekend, or styling your clothes a little differently) and then looking gently at how you feel afterwards. If you feel worse after making a small change, you can always change things up again, because this is an experiment that you can't fail. When you feel more able to make smaller decisions, ramp it up a little and see how it goes. You can go at your own speed, but it can be helpful to keep pushing just a little until you feel capable and happy when making change.

Social Stigma Is Exhausting

Dealing with stigma – a combination of labelling, stereotyping, separation, status loss, and discrimination (Link and Phelan 2001) – is a part of life for most trans people. Dealing with the pressures of oppression can be really physically, emotionally, and cognitively exhausting. It's okay if you feel the stigma of being trans and/or non-binary getting on top of you. It doesn't make you weak to be hurt by hurtful things – it only makes you human. After you've experienced a stigmatizing event, or been made aware of oppression happening in your community, it's okay to take all the rest you need and to concentrate on things that help you to feel safe and in control.

Rest and resilience may be the key to recovery from social stigma. While the current societal transphobia we experience never goes away, you can build a practice of self-care, including nurturing relationships and being part of your community, to help you feel more resilient. Resilience works on intrapersonal (within yourself), interpersonal (between yourself and other people), and community-based (with other people like you) levels, and connecting with these aspects of your life can make you feel stronger and more able to take on the world. Notice which aspects of your life make you feel less alone, more energized, and more whole, and make space for these things in your routine.

If you're also worried that social stigma will get worse if you're not actively resisting oppression all the time, it's okay to cut yourself some slack. The cliché that you can't pour from an empty cup is a cliché for a reason! While we work together to end transphobia, it is important to rest and recover when you find yourself hurting. It's okay to let the rest of the community take up the slack for as long as you need. There's little point in working to end oppression against trans and/or non-binary people if they're not around to enjoy it, and that includes you.

What Are Your Conditions of Worth?

Carl Rogers described our conditions of worth as our integrated external ideas about who we should be and how we should act if we want to be 'good', 'normal', and 'worthwhile' (Rogers 1959). We learn from a young age what pleases the people around us and it's natural to want to make others happy and to want to fit in to the world around us, so we take these ideas onboard and make them ours.

If our internal thoughts and feelings about how we can live our best life differ from what we've been taught gives us worth, this sets up an incongruence, which is an uncomfortable and often painful conflict within ourselves and/or with society. For example, if the people who raised you taught you when you were young that it's good to win, and reacted negatively to you when you didn't win a competition or game, you might find yourself panicking about the idea of being seen to be a 'loser' as an adult. Another example might be that you were praised for acting in ways that were seen as normal for your assigned gender at birth and discouraged from acting in ways that were seen as abnormal or unexpected for your assigned gender at birth, meaning you might feel confusion or shame around certain aspects of transitioning to become your authentically gendered (or agender) self.

These lessons can be direct – for example, a parent telling you that it is wrong to be trans – or indirect – for example, watching TV programmes where trans-coded people were laughed at for existing as themselves. Everybody has these introjected conditions of worth, and it is not necessary to try to get rid of all of them if they align congruently with how you see yourself. For example, if the adults in your life showed interest in what you had to say when you were young, you are more likely to grow up to believe that what you say is worth listening to, and this is a belief that you will want to hold on to because it is true. A lot of conditions of worth, like many complex parts of your personality, have facets that are worth keeping and aspects that can be let go of if they do not serve you.

Your individual conditions of worth – the parts of your life and personality that make you feel worthy or worthless – will directly affect your self-esteem, which will, in turn, affect several aspects of your experiences with depression. If you feel like who you are and what you do makes you worthless, it can be very easy to sink into depression.

It can be useful to spend some time paying attention to your thoughts and beliefs and explore, with compassionate curiosity, if they serve you. It can be helpful to use a journal for this, but you don't have to. Depending on how much time you have to commit to this, or how you tend to focus best, it can be worth either checking in with yourself periodically through the day or setting aside a certain amount of time to really listen to your thoughts. When a thought about yourself comes up, take a deep breath and really think about if that thought is helpful for you. Would you have these thoughts about someone else in your position? Does the thought make you feel worse about yourself or better about yourself? Is the language used in the thought insulting, kind, or neutral? Can you place where these thoughts are coming from in your life?

If you find yourself with an incongruent condition of worth – that is, if you find yourself with a belief about your worth that you've internalized and that you don't think is good for you – you've already begun the process of releasing it by recognizing that it is there. When this condition of worth comes up again for you, remind yourself that this belief isn't yours – it was given to you, and you can throw it away. Remind yourself that you are actually worthy of respect, of love, and of happiness, just by being you.

Make a Self-Esteem Chart

If you are depressed – especially if you're experiencing dysphoria, learned helplessness, social stigma, or wonky conditions of worth – chances are you see yourself as worthless. You may believe that you lack intelligence, that you are a failure, that you are unlovable, that you are ugly, or that you don't deserve to be happy. This is your depression lying to you.

A helpful strategy might be to make a pie chart (or any kind of chart, or even just a list – the pie chart just looks slightly more visually appealing, even if you're like me and you can't draw a circle) of things that give you self-esteem. You can fill it with anything that makes you feel okay and that feels important to your identity. This might include content like your family, your hobbies, things you've made, your job, how you look, your future goals, aspects of your transition, things you do in the community – or, if all of that is too much right now, it might be smaller things, like that you've washed your face every day this week or that you really like your hair sometimes. Whatever makes you feel even slightly good about yourself can go in the pie chart, with a bigger slice of the pie for the bigger feelings of self-esteem or happiness. Take a look at each slice and give each one some more thought. If there's something that brings you a large amount of comfort that you don't get to do very often, is there a way of bringing that into your life more fully right now? Is one of the slices something that also hurts you or that might be unhealthy, and can you find that same feeling in a different way – for example, if your family bring you comfort but also misgender you, can you spend more time with people who see you for you?

You can bring out this chart whenever you're feeling worthless or depressed about who you are, and you can see first-hand everything that you think is great about yourself. The good in you will be there to see in a brightly coloured circle, or in a long list, or scribbled on an old envelope. These things about you are so important and so worthy of admiration, and you can be sure there'll be more to come.

It's worth revisiting this every so often to see how your chart changes over time and with your general mood; what brings you comfort when you're sad may not bring you comfort when you're angry, for example.

Challenge Your Critical Inner Voice

Most people have an internal monologue, where a voice like yours verbalizes ideas and narrates events in your head. Part of this experience may involve having a critical inner voice, which may either be part of your usual inner monologue or slightly separate. Your critical inner voice is the negative part of your thoughts that says hurtful things when you make a mistake, says you're not good enough, or says you don't deserve to be yourself in the world. These negative thoughts are often introjected from people who treated you poorly in the past, particularly in childhood.

It might take you a long time and a lot of work to realize all of the ways your critical inner voice is speaking to you. Sometimes, it can be so deafening that it ruins your day; sometimes, your critical thoughts can be so sneaky that you're surprised when you realize how negatively you've been talking to yourself. Try to pay attention to the way you're speaking to yourself and give that negative voice an answer. The replies to this voice don't have to be positive if that's not how you're feeling – a neutral truth can be just as powerful as something upbeat. For example, if you look in the mirror and your inner critic pipes up to say, 'I look ugly,' you might counter this with, 'That's not true, that's just what someone told me once,' or, 'I actually think my hair looks great today,' or 'I'm not here to be looked at, I'm here to enjoy my day.'

If your critical inner voice is loud, it pays to have an equally loud 'cheerleader' voice. This can be a part of you that celebrates your victories, that is excited for what you do for yourself every day, and that says kind things to you through everything. You can find this voice within yourself or create it consciously – either way, you will need to work hard to make sure this inner voice is loud, clear, and speaking to you often. This can be something that you practise by inwardly celebrating when things go right, and consciously saying kind things to yourself when you know you would otherwise be critical. Let the part of you that loves you get loud!

Gratitude

A lot of people seem to struggle with the idea of gratitude as an exercise, so I want to share that I used to really struggle with it, too. When I was very depressed and my therapist recommended the practice to me, I thought the idea was much too cheesy to be helpful. It was also difficult to think of anything I was actually grateful for – depression makes it very difficult to see these things, and the circumstances of my life meant there wasn't much to be grateful for. I can remember lying in the dark in my cold and dingy house I could barely afford to rent, and running over the things I should be grateful for: there was a roof over my head; I had £2 for the bus to work that day; I wasn't dead. It didn't feel like much but, the more time and effort I was able to invest in the practice, the more things I could think of. After a while, I found I could focus on a few specific things that I was genuinely grateful for in a day: my friend had made me laugh at a really silly joke and it reminded me that I was a likeable person who knew cool people; the clothes I was wearing felt particularly physically comfortable, giving me a little burst of gender euphoria; the sunrise had been a particularly beautiful shade of pink, and I'd been able to stop for a minute to watch the colours slowly change in the sky. This kind of small, everyday gratitude was hard won but ultimately a factor in lifting me slowly from the depth of my depression.

Each individual experience of gratitude, no matter how small or how cheesy, builds upon others to create a greater sense of self-transcendence in your life (McCullough, Tsang, and Emmons 2004) and to slowly lift you out of depression. It can be helpful to keep some kind of gratitude journal, whether this is a dedicated list in a fancy journal, a note you write every so often in your diary, or a running list that you keep in your phone. If you decide to keep a list, you can always revisit what made you feel grateful in the past and remember times when things seemed a little brighter than usual, building up a memory bank of good times – something that depression often takes from you.

When you think about what makes you feel grateful, it can help to be as specific as you can. Being specific about what you're grateful for has multiple benefits: it reminds you that there are lots of things in life to be grateful for; specificity can help you to process life events; and you may be more able to remember uplifting events in your life when you look back on what you can be grateful for. For example, if today you are grateful that you have a roof over your head, it might be more helpful to think about why you're particularly grateful for that, perhaps because your bedroom gave you a safe and quiet place when you needed it today or because you were able to cook something you like to eat in your kitchen.

It might also be helpful to express your gratitude to others. Sharing your gratitude with those who make you feel good can help you to process that life is good while giving you the added boost of knowing you've made someone else's day a little brighter. Be grateful to yourself, too. Take some time to look at yourself and your life, and admire how far you've come and everything you've learned.

If you're into breathing exercises, here's a great one from Deb Dana's *Polyvagal Exercises for Safety and Connection: 50 Client-Centred Practices* (2020): breathe in with a word that acknowledges a moment to be grateful for and then breathe out with a word that expresses your gratitude. For example, if you're grateful for a lovely day of being with friends, you might breathe in while thinking the word 'friendship' and breathe out while thinking the word 'love'.

If, after this, you find yourself still not feeling good about gratitude practices (like I used to), that's totally okay! There is no one path or one set of skills that works for everyone, and you're not doing anything wrong if this doesn't work for you.

Engaging with Hope

Almost by definition, depression can make you feel hopeless. It can be so difficult to find any hope at all when you're feeling depressed, but it can be an important resource to cultivate if you can (Yip and Tse 2019). Holding on to the hope that you can achieve your goals can be a powerful way to work through depression (Li *et al.* 2018), including goals that prioritize your mental health and actualizing tendency (Acharya and Agius

2017). Hope can be an important catalyst for change and for recognizing where you really want to be in life. The more you can view your future self positively and your future world with hope, and understand that this future self is *you* and that this future world is *this* world, the easier it is to get to that hopeful place (Sokol and Serper 2017).

Maybe take some time to think about the aspects of your past, present, and future that make you feel hopeful right now. It's okay if you find this difficult – try to be compassionate with yourself and take your time. Things that make you feel hopeful might include: things you know you can already do, whether those are big or small things; doing things that you're good at; your spirituality; your family and your relationships; the children in your life; your community; good news about the world; being in new or favourite places; and future plans and goals. How can you incorporate some of those things into your day? How can you build more of these things into your routine?

Anxiety

In this chapter, we'll explore issues like how anxiety might feel to you, why transitioning might make you anxious (even when you know it's right for you), how to feel grounded and stay present when you're anxious, and how to listen to your anxiety without feeling overwhelmed.

What Is Anxiety?

Disordered anxiety is defined as excessive and uncontrollable worry about current and future events and activities that leads to restlessness, agitation, fatigue, difficulty concentrating, irritability, panic, physical tension, insomnia, and distress (American Psychiatric Association 2013).

Anxiety can look a number of different ways and it can affect so many different types of people. It can manifest as a feeling of unease, dread, worry, fear, or panic. It can be very difficult to relax your body and mind. You may feel continuously unsafe – from an unknown source, from a future or possible source, or because you are currently in an unsafe environment.

When anxiety becomes severe it may lead to an anxiety attack or panic attack, when someone begins to hyperventilate (breathe very quickly), feel sick, become dizzy, shake, dissociate, become hot and cold, feel nauseated, temporarily lose their sight and hearing, have tingly skin and extremities, and possibly feel faint. Anxiety can also manifest as irritability, a temper, snapping at others, feeling upset with yourself, or 'flying off the handle' when you feel overwhelmed.

Anxiety can be caused by many things. As a trans and/or non-binary person, you may be feeling anxious about coming out or being outed, how you have been or will be treated by others, how the current political landscape affects you, and any number of other things. About 80% of young trans people (Lough Dennell, Anderson, and McDonnell 2018) and 75% of adult trans people (McNeil *et al.* 2012) report symptoms of anxiety. With the changes, pressures, excitement, and dangers that often come with being transgender and/or non-binary, it's not a surprise that so many of us feel anxious, whether that's something we experience from time to time or 24/7.

Visibility and Anxiety Through Transition

All change can cause anxiety, even when the change is highly positive. Changes in relationships, how you relate to the world, and how the world relates to you are likely to be happening as you move through life as a trans and/or non-binary person. Over a third of trans people have reported that they avoid presenting how they would truly like to, due to the anxiety of being stared at, harassed, or assaulted (FRA 2012) – including me. Three out of four trans people are also too anxious to go to certain places for fear of being attacked in some way for being trans (FRA 2012).

Many of us face the anxiety of being both very visible and unseen in society. Many trans people find themselves to be highly visible in society, and being highly visible usually makes anxiety worse, especially when you have come to associate how visible you are with how much danger you could be in. On the flip side of the trans experience, feeling like you're invisible can also be a huge source of anxiety, especially when it comes to the type of invisibility that trans people often feel – like they are being purposefully ignored. Being part of an oppressed group can cause people to feel both hypervisible and invisible at the same time. You may feel that you're moving through the world with everybody staring at you, expecting certain things from you, and getting ready to hurt you, while never being seen for who you really are or being offered the opportunities that you deserve. Feeling hypervisible and invisible, whether separately or together, added to the other types of trauma that can come with being transgender, can lead to hypervigilance (a heightened alertness and watchfulness for danger, even in safe environments). These traumatic experiences all add up and may combine to make you feel overwhelmed and unsafe in the world.

Hypervigilance and How to Feel Safe Without Being Tense

Hypervigilance is the experience of being very alert and sensitive to your surroundings, usually with a sense of fear or anxiety and thoughts that you are unsafe. This might feel like being on edge all of the time, feeling like you're unable to switch off, getting overwhelmed easily when lots is going on around you, jumping or reacting to very small things, or feeling like your body can't rest even when you know you're safe. You might find yourself always looking around you and always aware of what other people are doing. You might find yourself jumping or flinching at any loud noise or sudden movement, and you might find yourself overwhelmed in noisy or crowded environments. You might find it difficult to fall asleep or to relax, even when you are physically comfortable and alone. You may find you cannot let your guard down or close your eyes in front of others, even people you love and trust. It might feel extremely important to you to feel as safe as possible at all times. When you can finally relax a little, you might find yourself exhausted. Hypervigilance is essentially the physical and emotional feeling that you cannot relax, often because you feel like danger can strike at any time.

People who experience hypervigilance have usually experienced trauma in their lives (van der Kolk 1997). This book's chapter, *Trauma*, offers more of an explanation but, in summary, by trauma here I mean both intense events, such as violence, and more insidious events, such as being misgendered. Hypervigilance is often a result of dealing with stress or trauma, either acute or experienced over a long period of time. It's often an extension of hyperarousal, where your body becomes continuously (and exhaustingly) prepared for trouble at any given moment (Krupnik 2021). If you have just been in a fight, for example, you might find yourself looking over your shoulder and feeling your heart hammering long after the argument is over. If you've faced microaggressions and transphobia over a long period of time, your brain will try to keep you safe by watching out for any danger or oppression as often as it can to try to protect you.

Hypervigilance can be useful. For example, if you're trying to escape a dangerous situation, being extremely aware of your surroundings can help you to defend yourself and escape. As useful as this can be, over a long period of time this constant awareness of your environment can leave you feeling drained and exhausted. When hypervigilance continues after the immediate threat is long past, it can leave you feeling anxious and burnt-out instead of being useful in helping you. Unfortunately, facing the threat of transphobia and microaggressions every day means you are often facing threats, and so hypervigilance can be a constant, anxiety-provoking, draining experience for many trans people.

Hypervigilance is a way that your body tries to keep you safe. If you're experiencing hypervigilance, you need some ways to feel safe and to remind yourself that you can keep yourself safe in the future. Swapping hypervigilance for appropriate vigilance at the appropriate time can be hard work, but will also help you to feel safe without exhausting yourself. I've found that a key component in this is self-trust; that is, knowing that you can take care of yourself in unexpected situations and that it is not your fault if you find yourself in an uncomfortable or troubling situation. Your hypervigilance wants to keep you safe by having you pay attention to everything in your environment, because at some point you have learned that danger can come from anywhere. It's important to intentionally remember that you have survived all of the dangers you have faced so far, no matter what direction the danger has come from. You can be prepared to take care of yourself without having to devote all of your time and energy to it. For example, if you're going out somewhere that doesn't feel safe, it might help to pinpoint some of the things that make you feel the most unsafe and come up with a plan to make these eventualities safer. You can plan the safest route in advance, plan for someone to go with you, make sure you've taken any necessary medication to reduce your anxiety, think about what you want to do if this event falls through, and run through the big things that will help to keep you safe.

When you start to think about the small stuff, it's okay to stop. You're going to be much better at thinking on the fly than you think you are! It might help to have a reassuring mantra, like, 'I'll know what to do,' or, 'I choose freedom over perfection.'

It's worth remembering that what feels like a big or small safety need will be up to you. For example, it might feel very unsafe to go to a restaurant without knowing what's on the menu, especially if you're neurodivergent or you have food intolerances, while for others this will not be something they even think about. It's okay to have different access needs to others!

Find a Safe Inner Place

It might help to have an internal safe place, as well as attending to your safety outside.

To find your safe place, take a deep breath, get comfortable, and imagine that you are somewhere safe. This place can be anywhere you like, but try to imagine somewhere different than where you live. It can be somewhere you've visited before, somewhere you've always wanted to go, or a completely new place that you've invented. Try to make sure there are no negative connotations in this place – it exists solely for you and your peace of mind, so, as opposed to all other elements of self-care that I recommend, there are only good vibes allowed here. You can give this place a name if you like. There's nobody else in this place; it's just for you, and it has all the features that you consider to be safe and secure.

Try to engage all of your senses when you think of this place. What colours, shadows, and textures can you see in the world around you? What can you feel with your hands, against your skin, underfoot? What does this place smell like, and do the scents change as you move around? What can you hear in the distance and close to you? Can you hear your own breathing and movements in this place, or is the environment too loud? Can you taste anything in the air or in the water as you explore? Is it daytime, night-time, or somewhere in between? What exactly is the weather like? What else is important about this place?

As you think about the environment you've created and the sensations you experience, pay attention to your physical body and how you feel. What can you notice about your breathing, your heartbeat, your posture, and your general levels of comfort?

You can explore and rest in this safe space for as long as you like, and you can also leave whenever you like. You can visit this place whenever you need a safe, calm space that's just yours. If you find that you need a moment to collect yourself, or that you need something safe to visualize when you're nearing a panic attack, your safe place will be waiting.

You Deserve to Feel Safe

What helps you to feel safe will depend on your past experiences and current situation. There are many ways to help yourself feel safe, including cognitively (e.g. reassuring yourself with evidence of your safety), emotionally (e.g. processing past events that made you feel unsafe), socially (e.g. making sure the people around you know and respect your boundaries), environmentally (e.g. making sure your living space is as clean and tidy as possible), and physically (e.g. using a weighted blanket or doing some deep breathing). It's okay to experiment with lots of things until you find what makes you feel particularly safe. It's also important to remember that you deserve to be safe, and to feel safe, all of the time, not just when you're feeling particularly rough, so it's good for you to regularly seek out things that make you feel safe, even when you're doing fine.

It can help if you set up a particular safe space in your living area that incorporates things that make you feel safe. This can be as simple or extravagant as you like. Depending on what helps you to feel safe, this might look like a large and open space or small, covered area. It can be helpful to experiment with the textures, scents, sounds, and temperature of your safe space. As you work on creating this space, think about all the things that make you feel like you deserve safety – even if it's just the universal idea that everybody deserves to be safe – and include related things in that space. Pictures of loved ones who want you to be safe, books about people changing the world for the better, and reminders of the amazing things you've accomplished can all be great additions to your safe space.

Mindfulness

Mindfulness is very much a buzzword right now. Over the past few years it seems to have become a major theme in wellness circles (Van Dam *et al.* 2018). This might have made you more eager to try it for yourself, or you might be facing some internal resistance because it's been overhyped. When used in a way that works for you, mindfulness can be very useful.

Mindfulness is a term for a set of techniques and practices that help you take inventory of how you're feeling and what you're thinking, with as little judgement as possible. This can involve anything from an hour-long mindfulness meditation to a stolen 30 seconds of paying attention to your breathing while you're taking a lunch break. The idea of mindfulness is: to notice each feeling, thought, and sensation that comes to you;

to look at what's happening right now without judgement; and to let it go.

If you're feeling particularly anxious, it might help to think of any unwelcome and overwhelming thoughts and feelings as a train. Get yourself as comfortable as you can and imagine yourself stood or sat on a train platform. As you notice yourself thinking and feeling, imagine those experiences as a train making its way to your platform. Take a look at the train and the thoughts and feelings you're experiencing – 'I'm starting to feel quite anxious,' for example, or, 'This is silly,' – and then watch the train slide past your platform and go on its way to some other destination. Sometimes, the same train is going to keep coming back to the station, and that's okay. Sometimes, you're on the train, and the train is on fire. That's okay, too. You can always get off at the next stop.

The way you visualize mindfulness can look any way that you like. As a therapist, I've helped clients sort thoughts neatly in boxes, shelve them in libraries, blow them into balloons and let them go, erase their words on paper, and place them gently on leaves to be carried away by a running stream.

Try to maintain a compassionate curiosity about yourself if your attempts at mindfulness seem to be going wrong. Your inner monologue, the part of you that talks to yourself, might be very negative if you feel that you're struggling with this. It's okay to answer that internal voice and ask gentle questions instead. For example, if you take a few minutes to try to still your thoughts and find it very difficult, you may feel angry and think something like, 'I'm too stupid to do this.' It's okay to recognize this thought, and purposefully think something like, 'When things are difficult for me, it doesn't mean I'm stupid. It might mean I need to practise this some more or visualize something else. Why does not being good at something right now make me feel angry with myself?' It's also okay if there's no answer to questions like that right now – it might just be useful to mull the question over gently for a while and then put it away.

If you're autistic or otherwise neurodivergent and you find you need to stim or fiddle while you practise mindfulness, that's also totally okay. Being still can help some people to concentrate fully, but if you're not one of those people and moving in any way helps you to concentrate, you should go for it. There are even ways to be mindful while walking, if you find being on the move helpful for concentration.

There's no wrong way to practise mindfulness and no wrong thoughts or feelings to have about it. If it's not for you, or you find yourself struggling, I promise you haven't failed. There's no way to fail in trying to look after yourself.

Grounding

When you're feeling anxious, it's probable that you also feel ungrounded. Techniques that seek to 'ground' you are designed to help you feel centred in your body and the present, and to reduce any aspects of anxiety that make you feel unfocused, like you're 'spinning out', or like everything's 'up in the air'.

Take a moment to stop what you're doing. Put a hand on your chest, if you can, and take a deep breath in through your nose. Let it out through your mouth, and then do that one more time. Unclench your jaw, relax your forehead, and let your shoulders fall back. Take another deep breath in through your nose and out through your mouth. Then, from the position you're in, try to find five things you can see, four things you can hear, three things you can feel, two things you can smell, and one thing you can taste (it's okay if you need to get up and move around a little to find something to smell or taste). Remember to keep breathing as you do this. This is called the 5-4-3-2-1 method of grounding.

Another technique to try is to centre yourself in your body. With your hand near your heart (or resting on your tummy if this gives you too much dysphoria), try to feel how your chest rises and falls with each breath. Try to be conscious of the way your skin touches other areas of skin on your body. Notice which parts of you touch the floor, or the furniture you're sitting on, and the air around you. Feel the weight of your clothes, your hair, your glasses, and any mobility devices you're using. Find the places in your body that feel tense or a little uncomfortable and adjust yourself slowly to see if you can change this. If you can, try to stretch a little in ways that feel comfortable when you're done. Noticing where and how your body is can help you feel more grounded in yourself, and this can help you to feel more present in yourself.

Please note that parts of this exercise may feel uncomfortable if you have certain sensory needs, so it's okay to choose what feels helpful to you and discard the rest.

If Grounding Triggers Dysphoria

Sometimes, trying to connect fully to your body can be a trigger for dysphoria, which can leave you feeling very ungrounded again, as well as causing other negative emotions. If this happens to you while you practise a grounding technique and it makes you feel a little uncomfortable, it might be worth staying with the uncomfortable feeling, looking at it gently, and trying to let it go as you continue with the grounding exercise. If this doesn't work, or if your grounding exercise makes you feel any more than a little uncomfortable, it's perfectly fine to stop. There will always be other exercises to try!

It's always okay to modify any self-care tips so that they fit with you and your needs. If putting a hand to your chest to feel your breath makes you feel chest dysphoria, for example, you can place your hand on your tummy. You can also try to concentrate on the feeling of your breath entering your nose and leaving your mouth instead – does the breath feel cold or warm? Is it easier to inhale or exhale? You could also try to focus on the feeling of your shoulders rising and falling – how much do they move when you breathe?

Find a Grounding Object

If you find yourself feeling ungrounded often, it might be worth keeping a small object with you that you find pleasant to touch. By small, I specifically mean something you can fit in one hand, or maybe two. It might also help if this object reminds you of a safe loved one or a calm memory. Objects that have worked for me and for my clients include painted stones, small soft toys, plastic dice, wooden toys, religious pendants, sturdy seashells, glass beads, lucky coins, and shaped metal tokens. One that I use is the small, inside doll from a matryoshka doll that was given to me by a treasured mentor as a reminder of my inner strength.

If you start to feel anxious or ungrounded, it can help to hold this object in your hand. What do you notice about how the object looks? Is it: bright or dark; colourful or muted; maybe a combination? What is the object made of? Notice the weight of it, the shape of it, and the temperature of it. How does it feel when you touch it in different ways? Does the temperature change when you hold it for longer? Does anything about it change when you hold it in your other hand? Hold it tightly (without hurting yourself) and keep it close to you until you're feeling more grounded.

You can return to your grounding object as often as you like, and you can have several grounding objects if you find that helpful. It can help to keep your grounding object in an easily accessible place, like on your desk or by your bed, or to choose something that's easily portable and can be worn or kept in a pocket (but if you decide to keep it in your pocket, be careful not to wash it!).

What Is Your Fear Telling You?

Anxiety is your body's way of telling you to be alert for danger. While anxiety can feel extremely unpleasant to say the least, it can help to remember that this is one of your body's many ways of trying to keep you safe. It can be an important part of your intuition – that is, your inbuilt ability to work out if things are unsafe or nonsensical.

It can be difficult, especially when you're very anxious, to tell which kind of fear you're feeling and what your intuition is trying to tell you (Remmers and Zander 2017). Is it the kind of anxiety where you can feel the fear and do it anyway, or should you listen to your gut and back away? While all anxiety is uncomfortable, it can be very useful to distinguish which thoughts and feelings might be useful and which might be harmful as you work through your anxiety.

When you find yourself feeling anxious but you're not sure what to do with it – for example, if you have a difficult decision to make and your anxiety is loudly confusing your ability to make a good judgement – it can be helpful to try to mitigate some of the physical feelings you're experiencing so you can more clearly see what's underneath. This generally involves looking after yourself in a way that lowers your heart rate and slows your breathing. This might involve breathing deliberately in through your nose and out through your mouth, making sure you're comfy and comfortably warm, talking to supportive people who make you feel calm, and taking in some soothing media. When you feel more physically settled, you can try to look at the difficult thoughts again while prioritizing your felt sense of safety. If your thoughts are still anxious while your feelings are less so, it can be worth looking at these thoughts in more depth to see if they're helpful to you.

It can also help to attempt to work out when your feelings are based – are your feelings based in what's happening right now, what has worried you in the past, or what could happen in the future? If you find yourself worrying about something that's happening now, it can be worth taking a step back and seeing how you feel after a break and a few deep breaths. You might find that your anxiety turns into anticipation, excitement, or resolve when you feel more physically centred – or you might not. If you find that your anxiety has been triggered because of a past event, spend some time reminding yourself that this is a new situation in a new time and that you are now safe. If you're worrying about what might happen in the future, it can help to look at what is likely to happen and try to put away the least likely consequences while you decide what to do. You can always take a look at any unlikely catastrophic thoughts later when a healthy decision has been made.

This can take a really long time to learn, and your sense of what anxiety is useful or unhelpful may never be 100% accurate. It can sometimes be helpful to talk about your anxiety and what you might be anxious about with a trusted friend or mental health professional, or to keep a journal, depending on how you tend to process your thoughts best.

Your Optimal Window of Tolerance

One way to work with your anxiety, instead of against it, is to think about your comfort zone, or your 'optimal window of tolerance' and how you tend to make your best decisions (Siegel 2010). This is the range of emotions and physical arousal (not the sexy kind – the kind that makes us feel awake, alert, calm, or depressed) that make it easier for us to learn, plan, take measured risks, make changes, and act. The idea of the window of tolerance is that it is a way of looking at how we're able to function when we're feeling good, and also how we're able to live good lives when feeling intense emotions. Everybody's window of tolerance is different, based on aspects of their life, such as personality, circumstances, and physical ability.

If you're able to, think of the intensity of your felt emotions on a scale of one to ten. One is, 'I'm too emotionally numb to do anything right now,' while ten is, 'I'm so emotional it feels like my body can't take it.' A three would be, 'I feel alert and very comfortable,' while eight would be, 'My emotions are intense, but if I take some deep breaths I can steady myself a little.' If you're feeling anxious, you might be anywhere between a four (slightly anxious) and a ten (having a panic attack). Trying to push through your anxious feelings if you're at an eight or above on this scale is likely to lead to an unenjoyable experience, maybe even a traumatic one. At points four to seven, you might be able to sit through your feelings of anxiety to examine the thoughts, physical feelings, and other emotions that come with it.

It's worth remembering that some people are going to hit

the seven on the scale much faster than others, while some people might find it difficult to get to a four on an ordinary day. Some people are also going to move from a four to an eight much more quickly than others, while some will need more time than others to distinguish the whats, whys, and hows of their anxious thoughts and feelings. However fast or slowly you become anxious, there's no shame in how you process your feelings.

Imposter Syndrome and Anxiety (Yes, You Are Trans Enough)

A common experience in people with anxiety is imposter syndrome. This is when you doubt aspects of yourself and your life, and feel that it's only a matter of time before others begin to doubt these aspects of yourself, too (Clance and Imes 1978; Sakulku 2011). For example, you may feel that you are not good enough to do your job, even though you are well qualified for it, and you may worry that you will be fired; or you may have a reputation for being good at something in particular, and be anxious about making any mistakes in case someone catches you being less than perfect.

You may also experience imposter syndrome around your gender identity, which is a very common trans experience (Violet 2018). This may manifest as a small worry that occasionally pops up or as a prevalent and life-altering fear. You may worry, for example, that you do not experience dysphoria the 'right' way (or at all); you may worry that you don't look feminine, masculine, or androgynous enough to 'really' be your gender; or you may occasionally accidentally misgender or misname yourself out of habit. This can be compounded by the expectations of those around you, particularly by family members, other members of the LGBTQ+ community, and figures of authority at your gender identity clinic.

One thing that I think is worth remembering is that imposters don't get imposter syndrome. If you were really a 'gender fraud', you would be revelling in your purposeful deceit; instead, you're anxious about whether you're a good person. Having imposter syndrome about an aspect of your life is generally a sign that you're doing a pretty good job at it. Likewise, worrying about whether you're trans enough is a pretty universally trans experience, and it's actually an excellent sign that you are who you say you are! If you're a person who is not fully or only the gender you were assigned at birth, you're trans; and if you're trans, then you're trans enough. There is no right or wrong way to be a trans and/or non-binary person.

Self-Harm

In this chapter, we'll explore issues like the ways you might be self-harming intentionally or unintentionally, different ways self-harm can start (often as a coping mechanism), and new ways that you can care for yourself when you feel you actually deserve to hurt yourself.

What Is Self-Harm?

Self-harm can be defined as any deliberate action you do that is designed to hurt yourself. People often have the idea that there are specific ways to self-harm, and that these are the ways that 'count' as self-harm. Cutting your own skin, for example, is often cited as *the* way to self-harm. Many people harm themselves in other obvious ways like hitting themselves, biting themselves, scratching themselves, burning themselves, poisoning themselves, and punching hard objects.

In reality, there are many ways to self-harm, and many reasons for doing so. You may not even be aware that you are self-harming. Drinking or smoking enough that you are hurt emotionally, socially, financially, and physically might be an example of less obvious self-harm, especially because it can look like fun and sometimes make you feel good. Even so, if you continue to use substances even though they hurt you and disrupt your life, you may be self-harming.

Purposefully getting into fights with loved ones and strangers can also count as self-harm, as can sabotaging healthy life events. Another example might be having baths that are so hot they make you feel sick, having unsafe sex, driving recklessly, or exercising past the point of exhaustion.

Self-neglect also counts as self-harm. People tend to think of self-harm as a step you take to hurt yourself, but not taking steps to make yourself feel okay also counts. You might do this because you feel you're not worth the energy or effort of taking care of yourself and that you don't deserve care. This can look like letting yourself get too cold on purpose, not looking after any wounds or illnesses, or not eating when you're hungry to the point that it affects you emotionally, cognitively, or physically.

Negative self-talk can also be a factor of emotional self-harm. You might find yourself letting your critical inner voice, the part of your inner monologue that says negative thoughts about you, get louder and louder because you think what it's saying is true.

Self-harm can happen for numerous reasons. Usually, there is an aspect of coping with difficult and overwhelming feelings that you don't know how else to process, or expressing those feelings when you don't know how else to show them (Tantum and Huband 2009). Self-harming can temporarily make some people feel more in control of their feelings and their life, especially in situations in which they feel they have no control of their body – a common feeling for trans people. Self-harm can also be a maladaptive coping mechanism when someone needs distraction, relief, focus, or to be 'lost' in something. Someone may also harm themself if they feel they need to be punished or deserve to be in pain. On the flip side of this, someone may find themselves self-harming because they believe this helps them to feel more alive.

Around 60% of trans people report having self-harmed (Nottinghamshire Healthcare NHS Foundation Trust 2017; PACE 2015), with trans men seeming to be particularly vulnerable (Marshall *et al.* 2016). Bullying, lack of support, substance abuse, family problems, and feelings of depression related to being trans seem to be the driving forces behind the high rates of trans people who engage in self-harm (Butler *et al.* 2019; Taliaferro *et al.* 2019). If these are issues that you're experiencing, you're definitely not alone.

When Self-Care Becomes Self-Harm

Elements of self-care can, over time, become a way to self-harm. If an activity that once refreshed your energy and made you feel calm now makes you feel very anxious if you don't do it, for example, or if an engaging hobby is now very boring but you still invest a lot of energy into it because you feel guilty if you don't do it, you may be unintentionally self-harming.

A good example of this might be my previous relationship with exercise. Exercise can be very good for you in many ways, including giving a boost to your mental health, if you do it in a self-compassionate, physically boundaried way that you enjoy. In my mid-twenties, as part of my physiotherapy for a chronic back problem, I engaged in a gentle exercise programme that reduced my pain levels and increased my emotional and cognitive energy. This exercise was great self-care – until I started doing what many people do and began to push myself in ways that hurt me. I began working out after 14-hour night shifts when I was exhausted and working myself past any normal physical discomfort to the point of physical pain, sometimes leaving the gym shaking and nauseated. My original goal to have fun and strengthen my back was becoming overshadowed by my guilt at not working harder, a need for some control in my life that I didn't quite recognize at the time, and a sneaky idea that maybe I deserved the pain I was in for being 'unfit'. After some time, I realized that my self-care routine had become self-harm, and I managed to work out how to mitigate this self-harm and keep caring for myself. For me, this means consciously being gentle with myself, making sure I'm well nourished before and after I exercise, checking in with myself often to make sure I'm in a good place with my exercise, and only doing exercise that I find fun (except for my physio exercises for my back, which are boring but very necessary!).

In relation to trans-specific self-care, both tucking and binding are self-care activities that can become self-harm under certain circumstances. That is not to say that either tucking or binding are inherently harmful, particularly if done safely, but, like many otherwise benevolent self-care activities and coping mechanisms, they can devolve into harmful practices under certain circumstances. Tucking in order for a transfeminine person to achieve a flatter crotch shape, for example, can drastically alleviate bodily dysphoria, ease social dysphoria, and create euphoria about how you look. For some transfem people, tucking is needed in order to survive and thrive in the world. There are several very safe methods, including wearing specially made underwear. If you find yourself tucking past the point of discomfort because you feel you need to, or because how you look is more important than how you feel even in a safe environment, or you find yourself tucking in ways that are causing physical damage, this may be an element of self-harm. If you think tucking may have become self-harm for you, try to examine why – do you feel that you deserve to feel pain in the body parts that give you dysphoria? Maybe you feel that how you look to others is more important than the damage you could do to yourself? Perhaps you feel that you don't deserve to get rid of your dysphoria in a way that also makes you feel happy? When you've figured out the reason, you can use this as a way to figure out how to turn tucking into self-care again, by doing so in a way that fulfils all of your needs.

Binding can also apply as self-harm in the same way. Binding is both important and necessary for many transmasculine people, myself sometimes included, and there are many ways to bind safely to create gender euphoria and decrease gender dysphoria. Using inappropriate binding materials or a too-small binder, however, may improve how you feel about your body shape but induce a huge amount of physical harm to your skin, ribs, back, and lungs. If you are wearing your binder for more than eight hours a day, or past the point of discomfort, it's worth examining if this has become self-harm and how to turn this back into self-care. Try to compassionately examine why and how your binding became an avenue for self-harm and use this knowledge to flip it back to self-care.

Substance Misuse

Substances, such as alcohol and marijuana, can be coping mechanisms that we adopt at a time when nothing else can help. When we're facing the trauma of oppression and minority stress (Meyer 2003), substances can be both a release and an escape as we try to cope with the world (Stevens 2012; Nuttbrock *et al.* 2014; van Heugten-Van der Kloet *et al.* 2015). They can also help us to deal with dysphoria by providing a distraction, keeping us disconnected from our body, and numbing our emotions. This can be something that helps you in the short-term but can wildly increase your dysphoria and the effects of other traumas in the long-term. Reports have shown that around one in four transgender people misuse substances, compared with one in ten cisgender people (Hunt 2012). Trans people seem to have particularly high rates of alcohol, nicotine, and marijuana misuse (Reisner *et al.* 2015: Glynn and van den Berg 2017; Hughto *et al.* 2021).

For clarity, substance misuse is not the same as substance use – 'use' of a substance becomes 'misuse' when the substance is used in a way that it is not meant to be used, when it is used in excess, when there is a potential for harming yourself or others, or when using the substance interferes with your daily life. The substance itself can include any kind of drug, such as alcohol, nicotine, prescription drugs, over-the-counter medicines, illegal drugs, and even caffeine. Misuse can happen once, occasionally, or regularly. To help you consider if your substance use has tipped over into misuse, the most commonly used current diagnostic criteria for a substance abuse disorder (American Psychiatric Association 2013) are as follows.

- Taking the substance for longer than you're meant to, or in larger amounts.

- Wanting to cut down or stop taking the substance, but finding that you're unable to.

- Spending a lot of time and resources to obtain the

substance, use the substance, or recover after using the substance.

- Experiencing cravings for the substance or feeling like you need it.

- Not managing to complete important tasks in your daily life because of substance use.

- Continuing to use the substance, even after you've noticed it's causing problems in your life.

- Giving up important work, hobbies, relationships, or items because of substance use.

- Continuing to use the substance even if using it has put you in distressing or dangerous situations, maybe multiple times.

- Continuing to use the substance even when you know you have a physical problem, mental health issue, or transition-related concern that could be impacted by taking the substance.

- Noticing tolerance, where you need more and more of the substance to get the same effect as before.

- Noticing withdrawal symptoms when you stop taking the substance, which are only fully relieved when you use more of the substance.

While substance use may have helped you to cope with traumatic situations, substance misuse can, over time, make how you're feeling much worse. Substance use and misuse can affect our levels of concentration, our understanding of what is happening in the present moment, our connection with our bodies and emotions, our memory, our inhibitions, and our ability to process trauma – all of which are tempting as coping mechanisms but also suppress our ability to work through how we feel and what has happened to us so we can heal. Ultimately, the longer substances are used to mask a problem in our lives, the longer we will have to deal with the problem and the bigger the problem will become in our lives, often with the added physical and psychological ramifications that misused substances can cause. It's also worth remembering that, chances are, if your transition involves a medical component, substance misuse will have an effect on how medications and surgeries will go for you, a factor that is important to consider for your future happiness.

It can be a huge struggle to overcome substance misuse and to switch to healthier and more helpful coping mechanisms, but it is worth it. You might find it useful to keep track of your substance use and your mood, and to set specific and measurable goals for your recovery, while you engage in all the self-care that you can. In terms of caring for yourself, it may be worth prioritizing your most basic and important needs, such as food, hydration, physical safety, sleep, and general health (Maslow 1943), before moving on to working through different ways to cope with stress. Asking for support from as many people and places as you can is often very helpful, including from helping professionals like your doctor or the advisory help service FRANK (see the *Charities, Helplines, and Other Free Advice* chapter). If you're seeking therapy, finding a trans-friendly, trauma-informed, substance-use-knowledgeable therapist is going to be a must. Staying away from the people and places that encouraged you to misuse substances, and finding new sober communities, can be extremely helpful, especially if you can find other trans people who have also worked through substance misuse and with whom you can engage in mutual support (Hendricks and Testa 2012; Oggins and Eichenbaum 2002). Meeting with other trans people in sober settings in general can be an excellent way of meeting with other people while staying safe (Stevens 2012). Clients have told me that focusing on the road ahead and what they want their life to look like without misusing substances is a powerful force in helping them to heal.

Self-Sabotage as Self-Harm

Even good changes can be really scary to face, which can lead to purposeful or accidental self-sabotage (Boyes 2018). This is a kind of emotional self-harm that sabotages your chances of happiness, often because of fear and low self-esteem. It might look like breaking up with a partner because they make you 'too happy', turning down your dream job because you're too frightened to take it, or procrastinating on applying for something you really want because you're worried you'll fill out the application wrong. For trans people, this might look like procrastinating on ordering a blood test for your HRT even though you really want to keep taking it, lashing out at family members who affirm your identity in case things change in the future, or never trying on your new gender-affirming clothes because you 'just know' that you'll hate how you look in them. Self-sabotage can happen for a number of different reasons, but it tends to happen when you're facing life changes that worry or frighten you to the point of you feeling overwhelmed. This may be most apparent: when you're too frightened to act on something even though you know it will have a positive impact on your life; when good things start to happen and you feel like you don't deserve them; when you're worried that a change is 'too good to be true' or that you will get hurt down the line, despite evidence to the contrary; or when positive change happens and you think you may not be able to handle it. You might find yourself procrastinating, putting yourself down, or catastrophizing (imagining the worst possible outcome of a situation).

Self-sabotage is a defence mechanism and coping mechanism that may have kept you safe from disappointment in the past but will ultimately only keep you from growing (Bishop 2017). It's likely that this is happening because you have experienced trauma around growth and happiness in the past – and, if the past has been painful, it makes sense that this is what you have come to expect from the future. What, however, if the past does not repeat itself, and the future is actually amazing? What if you knock this out of the park, people are kind to you, and you get your happy ending? Or – what if it doesn't go as smoothly as you'd hoped, but that's still okay because you're a different, more capable person now, with lots of new resources for handling distress? It's okay to be afraid of important things, such as elements of your transition, but it's important to know how to move through this fear to the other side without hurting yourself in the process.

If you suspect that you might be sabotaging something potentially great in your life, set aside some time to look at the issue and be compassionately curious about it. What do you think you're currently sabotaging, and why? What emotions do you feel when you think about it? Is it easy to look at, or do you find yourself wanting to think of something else or block out your feelings? Remind yourself that sabotaging your success is not actually protecting you – moving forward through your negative feelings will. From there, you can make a plan of action to set out some positive changes that can help you to feel excited as well as scared and keep talking to yourself and treating yourself in self-supportive ways. Remember that things don't have to be perfect – as a mentor once told me, if it's worth doing, it's worth doing badly. It can also be really helpful to share these thoughts and plans with trusted people in your life so that they can reassure you and cheer you on. Let yourself win!

Self-Care for When You'd Rather Self-Harm

When you feel the urge to self-harm, you may need a specific kind of self-care that meets the need self-harming would have met. Take some time when you're feeling particularly calm to consider how you feel and what your thoughts are when you feel the need to self-harm, and try to identify what makes you feel like self-harming. Do you feel panicky, angry, numb, desperate, disgusted? Where are these feelings directed – inwards towards yourself, outwards towards someone else, or towards the world in general? Are you having any physical sensations, like feeling your heart beating hard, feeling numb inside, or feeling like you want to cry? Try to think of how you can lessen this feeling and meet the need it brings.

I've collated a few examples of self-care by how you might feel when you're self-harming or about to self-harm. It can be helpful to familiarize yourself with a few of these ideas so that you remember the suggestions when you're next about to self-harm. These techniques are designed to help you feel calmer and more in control, and they have aided many of my clients, but it's important to note that, due to their connection with self-harm, they could also be a trigger for self-harm itself.

I would advise you to be as mindful as possible when trying out these techniques and to offer yourself compassionate curiosity if things don't go as planned. If these ideas don't work for you, you can use them as a jumping-off point to try to think of ideas that might be more helpful for you. You might also find that what you need changes over time and that's okay, too.

For when you're feeling overwhelmed and need a way to process your feelings: Do some deep breathing, splash your face and hands with cold water, write down how you feel, draw how you feel, cancel or postpone what you don't need to do, use a grounding object, ask for help.

For when you feel you're not worth the effort of caring for yourself, and that you don't deserve care: Talk to a trusted person, wrap yourself in blankets, concentrate on your breathing, cut your nails, have a warm bath (not too hot), care for any body mods, think of things you're good at, let others take care of you for a while.

For when you feel you need to be punished or that you deserve to be in pain: Eat something, drink something non-alcoholic, remind yourself of good things you've done, talk or write compassionately to your critical inner voice, care for a pet, draw marks where you usually self-harm (on your skin or on photos).

For when you feel you need to express or release negative feelings: Scream, cry, talk to someone you trust, hit safe objects (like cushions), throw objects onto a sofa or bed, write how you feel on your skin, bite something safe (like a stim toy), rip up something unimportant, breathe deeply.

For when you're looking for ways to control your feelings, your body, or your life: Make small decisions, move around, change your scenery, clench each part of your body in turn and then relax, plan something for the future, tell someone your future plans, make something, write affirmative words on your skin.

For when you need a distraction or want a way to turn your feelings off: Listen to loud music or white noise, shout how you're feeling, do something with your hands or body, try a safe-place visualization, play a video game, go for a brisk walk, ask a loved one about their day, write a fictional story.

For when you want to feel alive and you're looking for a 'rush' or an escape from numbness: Scream, dance to angry music, stomp around, tear up something unimportant, hold ice cubes in your hands (but let them go when they hurt), splash your face and hands with cold water, eat something minty, smell something with a strong and pleasant scent, move your body.

Finding a way forward through self-harm is such a hard thing to do and it's okay if this is too hard sometimes. Although you never deserve to be harmed, you're also not a bad person for hurting yourself or for not being able to care for yourself perfectly in the moment. If you're finding it hard to care for yourself right now, that's because it is hard, and you're doing something wonderful when you try.

Body Image

In this chapter, we'll explore issues like what an unhealthy body image might look like, how our bodies are meant to change over time, what nourishing your body really means, and ideas about how to deal with dysphoria in healthy ways.

What Is Body Image?

Everybody has a body image. Your body image is how you think about your body, and how you presume others think about your body. This might relate to how your body looks, what your body can do, the size and shape of your body, your perception of your own attractiveness, how you think about your gender in relation to your body, and whether you experience gender euphoria and/or dysphoria around parts of your body.

Your body image can be affected by so many things, especially as a trans and/or non-binary person. Depending on how you tend to think about your trans identity, thinking about your body may make you feel many things, from joy and freedom as you explore your gender and how you want to look, to disgust and shame as you deal with dysphoria and internalized trans-phobia. Your body is also likely to be under a lot of scrutiny from yourself and others as a trans person, causing you to think a lot about how you are perceived by other people.

Your experience of thinking about and inhabiting your body is likely to change as your body, thoughts, and circumstances change through your lifetime, and especially as you transition in different ways (McGuire et al. 2016) Young trans people seem to be particularly susceptible to unhealthy body image, with a higher chance of developing disordered eating than their cis peers (Connolly et al. 2016). Body dissatisfaction tends to be higher in people who want medical gender reconstructive treatments and haven't received them yet (Owen-Smith et al. 2018). Binary and non-binary trans people who report that they have faced harassment or rejection also report lower levels of body appreciation, reduced self-esteem, and lower satisfaction with life in general (Tabaac, Perrin, and Benotsch 2018).

What Does Unhealthy Body Image Look Like?

A body image becomes unhealthy when it goes from positive or neutral to negative or distorted, particularly when you believe that you are not good enough in some way because of your body's appearance or capabilities.

If your body image is unhealthy, you might find yourself thinking about how your body looks to other people often, and feeling shame or disgust about your body. You might also find yourself 'body checking', which is looking closely at parts of your body to see if there is any change or to inspect the aspects of yourself that you don't like (Shafran et al. 2004; Walker, White, and Srinivasan 2018).

If you have dysphoria around your body, your face, or aspects of what your body can do, you're also more likely to have a poor body image (Becker *et al.* 2018). You may find yourself looking at body parts you hate in the mirror, picking out facial features you wish you could change, comparing your shape and size to those of other people, thinking derogatory comments about your body, criticizing your body out loud to others, or thinking you should look like people you see in the media.

Dealing with Dysphoria in a Way That's Healthy for You

When you're working on your body image and how it ties in to your dysphoria, and vice versa, there are lots of body-based self-care ideas that you can consider.

Setting boundaries around how people describe or talk about your body can be really important in dealing with dysphoria. You might find it useful to let the people in your life know what gendered compliments feel good to you and which ones don't (e.g. you can let your loved ones know how you feel about being called handsome, pretty, or cute), and which body parts make you feel dysphoric and euphoric (e.g. it might trigger your dysphoria if friends tease you about your shoe size, or it might make you feel euphoric if a lover comments on the length of your hair). You can also set social and personal boundaries around what makes you feel best and worst in your body (e.g. you can let your loved ones know that invitations to go swimming currently make you feel dysphoric, but you'd love to be invited for another kind of gentle exercise next time).

Expressing your dysphoria and euphoria, subtly or loudly,

with your body can be an excellent way to deal with it. Lean into clothing styles and fashions that always make you feel great when you wear them. Show off your body parts or facial features that make you feel strong, grounded, and joyful in your gender. Wear pronoun badges with pride. If you can, show some extra physical care to the body parts or features that make you feel dysphoric – they're the parts that are so often ignored, and ignoring your body can hurt you in many different ways.

Remember that you don't have to love, or even like, how your body looks and works to have a healthy body image. You can care for who you are and what you look like now, and all the possible ways you might look in the future, without thinking you look great or while experiencing dysphoria. Loving yourself and your current body means knowing that you are good despite your dysphoria; that you are good despite feeling bad. Try to remember that your body will always be yours, no matter what it looks like, but you are not just your body – there are so many other important things about you.

Ultimately, transitioning in the ways you want to, away from any dysphoria and towards gender euphoria, is likely to increase your self-esteem and body satisfaction (Gleming et al. 1982), as well as improve your mental health in general (Gómez-Gil et al. 2012; Mueller et al. 2016) and your general quality of life (Simbar et al. 2018).

If these ideas don't work for you, remember that you haven't failed anything or done anything wrong. Everybody has different experiences of dysphoria, and everybody deals with their dysphoria differently. What's healthy for you and how you handle your dysphoria might look totally different from how another person handles their dysphoria, and that's okay – your needs are unique. You can always adapt anything here and experiment with what feels like healthy self-care for you.

Body Change, Both Fast and Slow

Your body is likely to change over time. This may be because of medical transition, but also because of the effects of social transition, aesthetic choices, ageing, pregnancy, disability, and other life events. Many of these changes will happen gradually and cumulatively, while some will happen suddenly. Some of these changes will come and go, while others will be permanent. All of these kinds of changes can feel positive, negative, neutral, or a mixture of all three, and you may find your thoughts and emotions about these changes shifting over time.

It's also okay if your body changes more slowly or more quickly than you'd like during your transition. That is not to say that it will always *feel* okay, but to remind you that it's normal and healthy for your body to do what it needs to do, even if that isn't what you had planned. For example, if you plan on taking HRT as part of your transition, it is normal for some changes to happen very quickly and for some to happen very slowly, and for this speed to be completely out of your control. You might also find that the changes you're most worried about, or that you feel most neutral about, are the first changes to appear. Another example I hear about from clients is the frustration of the long healing period after gender reconstruction surgery (e.g. top surgery, bottom surgery, and facial feminization surgery). Many people experience excitement and peace after these surgeries but also feel anxious and disappointed when there is so much aftercare to do and so much time needed to heal before fully enjoying the freedom offered by their reconstructive surgeries.

Whether you're going through a fast change or a slow change, it's important to take a moment or two when you can to check in with yourself and ask yourself how you're feeling about it. Depending on how you like to process things, you might find it useful to write a journal entry, doodle how you're feeling, make a video or voice note, or just think about it in a comfortable place. If a change has been on your mind lately, it can be helpful to hold on to that thought for a moment and take a deep breath. Ignoring how you 'should' or 'ought to' feel, what are your current emotions about this change? Have you noticed how you tend to think about this change or how you tend to talk about the changing body part? Does this change mean you need to alter your behaviour to be comfortable (e.g. does a change in your pain levels mean you need to change the way you move your body?), or does it change your needs in any way (e.g. does a change in your body shape mean you need new clothes that fit you?)? No matter how you feel emotionally about this change, can you accommodate for it in a way that improves your life (e.g. if you are taking testosterone as part of your transition and you find that this is giving you acne, you may feel shame about this but still commit to caring for your skin and continuing to take your testosterone regularly)?

These fast and slow body changes happen to everyone at every stage of life. Remember that your body is supposed to change, to grow, and to transition in so many ways as you navigate life. Your body will change as you go through life, presenting lots of new opportunities to care for yourself.

Controlling an Unruly Body While Avoiding Disordered Eating

Trans and/or non-binary people are more likely than cis people to have disordered eating behaviours and diagnosed eating disorders (Harrison 2019; Vocks *et al.* 2009). Disordered eating is often about control (Wagner, Halmi and Maguire 1987; Froreich *et al.* 2016) and, if there's one thing dysphoria can do, it's make you feel like you're not in control of your body. To cope with those thoughts and feelings, you may find yourself trying to control your body in ways that may not be healthy. This can include not eating enough, eating until you're in physical pain, only letting yourself eat certain things, measuring your food intake with the aim of intentional weight loss, exercising until it makes you ill, taking laxatives with the aim of intentional weight loss, making yourself sick, or taking diet pills.

There can be a lot of pressure for trans people to 'perform' gender correctly, and this almost always means there is pressure to conform to thinness. This thinness will look different depending on your gender, from the slim waist and managed curves that are expected of women, to the skinny, flat-chested androgyny expected of non-binary people, to the lean muscles and slight hips expected of men. Of course, this isn't how gender or bodies work, so your body is unlikely to fit these unhelpfully narrow expectations (which would also be true if you were cisgender). With this oppressive expectation of thinness and derision of fatness from society, plus a desire for control of a body that you might not feel fully at home in, it's no wonder that so many trans people develop disordered eating patterns as a coping mechanism.

There's so much evidence to show that disordered eating, intentional weight loss, and appearance-focused exercise don't do your body or your body image any good (Campos *et al.* 2006; Neumark-Sztainer *et al.* 2006; Bacon and Aphramor 2011; Harrison 2019; Hobbes and MacKay 2018). Nourishment is important to help your body change in the ways it needs to, both to get through life and to get through transition. The only way that you can nourish yourself fully is to eat and drink enough. Part of controlling this aspect of your nourishment is by letting go of society's rules of how you are meant to look and what you are meant to eat. Instead, you can focus on choosing to eat regularly, choosing to listen to your body's cues, choosing what delicious things you're going to eat today, and choosing to be well nourished and hydrated to the best of your abilities. In doing so, you get to decide to be wholly yourself without exploitative cisnormative expectations affecting what, when, and how you eat. There is so much power in taking control of your body in this way! You may get bigger, or smaller, or stay the same, and this will be largely beyond your control, but you will gain the energy and the strength to make other decisions and other changes in your life.

There are also many other ways to feel in control of your body while making healthy choices. While what you do with your body will be influenced by your abilities, disabilities, and felt sense of safety, choosing to use your body in ways that make you feel good can be an excellent way to feel in control and grounded in your body. This might include whatever exercise makes you feel strong and connected to yourself, but it can also include any activity that uses your body in enjoyable ways – dancing around your kitchen, painting, knitting, playing a musical instrument, singing, baking, playing with your pets or children, getting intimate with someone, stimming – anything that puts your sense of self back in your body in a pleasant way might help.

Making controlled decisions about what goes on your body can also have a huge impact on how you feel about yourself. Medical aspects of transition aside, this can include temporary changes, such as clothes, make-up, and hairstyles, and more permanent changes, such as piercings, tattoos, and other body mods. The more permanent the change, the more consideration you might want to give to the decision, but these changes can all give you an empowering sense of control, which may make you feel anything from energized and powerful to calm and composed.

Whatever happens, remember that you need to eat. Having enough to eat is a basic human need, not an optional bit of self-care!

Nourishing Yourself Emotionally as well as Physically

Throughout your transition, and your life in general, it is important to pay attention to your nutrition. It is very important to your mental health that you get enough to eat and, by this, I mean that you eat what you want when you're hungry and that you feel comfortably full afterwards. If any diets or guidelines dictate what is enough to eat, and you are still hungry afterwards, you have not had enough to eat, and those guidelines are wrong for you (Bacon 2008). Being hungry, and experiencing any kind of deprivation or restriction, can heavily impact your mental and physical health (Harrison 2019). It's okay if this means your body changes and gets bigger – remember that your body isn't supposed to stay the same and is supposed to change as you expand your life. Nourishing your body is one step towards nourishing your whole self, and nourishing your life. Your body will need energy while you live your best life.

While you make sure you're getting enough nutritional energy for your body, it's also important to think about how much energy your mind is getting. In the same way that you'll feel calmer and more comfortable after a tasty and filling meal (Tandoh 2018), chances are you'll feel your best when you are emotionally, relationally, creatively, and spiritually energized.

During a quiet moment (whether this is a whole day or a stolen five minutes), it can be worth thinking about the attributes of your life that make you feel good about yourself, whether this relates to your body or to your life in general. A more focused way to think through this is to set a timer for about five minutes and list as many things that you can think of that make you feel great about yourself. This list can include aspects of your personality, parts of your body, accomplishments you're proud of, cool things you like to do, loving relationships you've forged, things you've created, teams you've joined, and happy memories you've made. When the timer is up and you've made your list, read through it and consider: what is it about these things that help you feel like your true self? Which of these things do you think help you to grow? You can keep this list to add to or to look at again, if that feels good to you.

Loving Yourself Enough to Change While Staying True to You

One of Carl Rogers' most cited quotes, including in this book, is, 'The curious paradox is that when I accept myself just as I am, then I can change' (Rogers 1961, p.17). Accepting yourself doesn't mean staying exactly as you are now forever. It also means accepting the changes that happen outside of your control, accepting the changes you want and need to make, and accepting your need to grow and shift.

Showing yourself self-compassion, even when you know you won't be this version of yourself forever, can be so important. Accepting yourself as you are does not mean you can't change, nor that you don't want to, it just means that, right now, you can accept your body the way it is. Accepting your current self and everything you currently need, do, feel, think, and want doesn't even need to feel good; it just means that you see yourself for who you are right now with as little judgement as possible. If you can give yourself what you need right now, to the best of your abilities, you are fuelling your life for the changes you want to make in the future. Approach what you believe needs to change about yourself with a compassionate curiosity.

Progress Isn't Always Pretty

Sometimes, when you change something in your life for the better, it doesn't look better. Sometimes, according to society, it can look worse. Progress in dealing with complicated emotions, for example, can mean looking vulnerable, sad, and angry – emotions that we're not supposed to have 'out loud' but which are essential for us to fully experience. Sometimes, learning to be physically healthy, such as recovering from disordered eating, can make us feel less conventionally attractive. Sometimes, transitioning will make us feel right and free, even if it doesn't make us look how we thought it would, and even if society says otherwise.

All kinds of emotions, and all kinds of change, are part of your progress through life towards better mental health. Sometimes, the change isn't going to be a pretty one; sometimes, the change is, itself, about learning to be comfortable with things not turning out how we picture them. Some of the very best things in life are messy and unconventional, like wonky home-made cakes, or a weathered hand-me-down from a family member, or that cute little imperfection on a loved one's face. These things can still be beautiful in their own way – including you.

Beauty Standards Suck

It's important to remember that the beauty standards that
are upheld in Western societies are based in colonialist, racist,
fatphobic, ableist, and queerphobic ideals that make it actively
hard to have a good body image (Daley 2021). When you remember this, I think it makes it easier to care less about whether
or not you're fitting these beauty standards – these standards
are designed to be damaging to you and others, so it's okay to
not meet them. While there are societal privileges associated
with being pretty, handsome, thin, or muscular, throwing the
rulebook out the window also grants you the privilege of not
giving a damn. When you don't have to fit in with anyone's ideals,
this can give you the space and the freedom to grow in exciting
new ways and to have fun with your body and presentation. Try
to hold on to the knowledge that you don't have to look like
anyone else's ideal of 'good' to be good and feel good.

You Are Wanted

Somebody, now and in the future, thinks you're the best person
in the world, despite what this often cruel and reductive society would like you to believe. There is someone out there who
loves – has loved, will love – someone exactly as you are. There
is no need to become smaller, transition in prescribed ways, or
hide fundamental parts of who you are so that others will like
you, because it is guaranteed that someone will look on your
idiosyncrasies with love. Many won't – to hell with them. There
are so many others who will see the whole of you, hurting and
stared at and complicated, and see someone beautiful in all

the ways that matter to you. There is no need to become 'easier' for the people who say they love you but then, through direct instruction or indirect behaviour, ask you to become less of who you are. You do not need to be trans in a way that is palatable to the world if that is not what you want or who you are. You are worthy of all the healthy kinds of attention that feel good to you, whether that's from one other person, or a hundred, or just from you (because you're deserving of the kinds of love you want, especially when you're asexual, aromantic, or just not feeling it).

I promise you're wanted. We're out there for you, waiting to see the whole of you, no matter what that looks like.

Dissociation

In this chapter, we'll explore issues like the different kinds of dissociation, what it's like to be part of a system of personalities, what you can do if you're experiencing depersonalization, how to cope if you feel numb, and how to deal with intrusive thoughts.

What Is Dissociation?

When something terrible happens to us, it's a very ordinary response to try to push the resulting memories and emotions away, whether this is your choice or something you feel is happening to you (Herman 1992). When something traumatic happens and it can't be processed, a disintegration happens – normal processes that are designed to keep you safe start to happen wonkily (Levy and Anderson 2008). You might remember a traumatic event but have no emotional attachment to it, for example, or feel strongly emotional while missing memories of the event. You might find yourself feeling numb when something intense happens to you, experiencing some lost time during an acute trauma, feeling disconnected from the present, or running on autopilot as you go about your usual routine. You might also find yourself thinking thoughts that don't 'feel' like you, feeling like you're not quite in your body, feeling like the people and phenomena in the world around you aren't quite real, or feeling like you're watching your life without experiencing it. You may also have gotten used to certain types of physical and emotional traumas to the point that you don't notice them any more (Hoffman-Fox 2017). All of these are examples of dissociation.

The most common types of dissociation that you are likely to experience are derealization and depersonalization (Jones 2017). Derealization is the dissociative feeling that you are not connected with the world around you to the point that your perception of the world seems to be distorted. Depersonalization is the dissociative feeling that you are not connected to your body or your sense of yourself (Jones 2018).

You may also feel like your body is home to multiple consciousnesses. This can feel and look multiple different ways (Ribáry et al. 2017). You may experience having dissociative identities – where different consciousnesses within you 'front' at different times – talking and acting while you sit back in your mind and watch, or maybe while you have no memories of them doing so. Instead of this, or as well as this, it may feel like there are multiple voices with different personalities talking in your head, having different opinions about what is happening around you at the same time. These different personalities can be traumagenic, coming into being because of traumatic events in your life, or they may not be (Ross, Norton, and Wozney 1989). These voices and personalities can take many different forms and have many different genders, even ones different from your own. They may also be different ages, have different sexual orientations, remember different life events, and fulfil different roles in your life (Ross *et al.* 1989). This is colloquially known as 'being part of a system' or 'being plural'. Dissociative Identity Disorder also falls under this category and is described as the presence of at least two or more distinct personality states with recurring periods of amnesia, which causes profound distress or impaired functioning (American Psychiatric Association 2013).

Research has shown that trans and/or non-binary people are more likely to experience dissociative disorders (Walling, Goodwin, and Cole 2015; Mun *et al.* 2020), with nearly a third of trans people meeting the criteria for a dissociative disorder (Colizzi, Costa, and Todarello 2015). Trans people who report experiencing trauma and transphobia (Keating and Muller 2019) as well as gender dysphoria (Jones 2017) show high levels of dissociation. Trans people in general are more likely to experience depersonalization – the feeling that your body isn't 'yours' in some way (Colizzi *et al.* 2015).

Am I Dissociating?

If you find yourself dissociating a little or a lot, you're not alone. Everybody dissociates to some degree and it's a totally normal experience.

Here are some experiences that might suggest you are dissociating.

- Feeling emotionally numb or detached from reality.

- Feeling physically numb or detached from your body.

- Finding yourself staring into space without thinking or being aware of your surroundings.

- Feeling as if you're watching yourself, like in a movie.

- Feeling as if your body is floating or feeling like your consciousness is floating above you.

- Feeling as if you're 'one step behind' your body and actions.

- Hearing or seeing what other people are saying but being unable to process their words or communication, as if they're very far away.

- Feeling like your body is dead, robotic, alien, ghostly, rotting inside, or otherwise doesn't really belong to you.

- Forgetting core information about your life, such as where you live.

- Experiencing physical symptoms of an emotion without feeling it, e.g. suddenly feeling your heart rate increase and your body tense with no known cause or emotion behind it.

- Talking to others about something you did together recently and not being able to remember the occasion.

- Losing time or 'blacking out' without the influence of outside factors like head injuries or medication.

- Continually finding marks on your body that don't seem to have any cause.

- Feeling like the 'real you' has been buried, pushed aside, or given a back seat while someone or something else is in charge of your body.

- Remembering recently doing an important task but not being able to remember how you did it or what you said, beyond blurry memories.

Everybody Dissociates

Dissociating is a normal way to cope with traumatic or overwhelming events, whether this is happening now or has happened in the past. This dissociation can be long-lasting, for example after a bereavement you may find yourself struggling to fully feel your grief until a while after the loss, or it can be acute, for example you may feel like you're watching yourself give an important and frightening presentation with little memory of what you said afterwards. Another ordinary and very common type of dissociation is 'going on autopilot', when you find yourself completing boring or repetitive chores with no conscious awareness – another part of you is taking care of the boring parts so you don't have to! This is a normal and common way for your brain to try to process uncomfortable feelings and information, and usually you will find another way to process the information that has been dissociated in time – the feelings of your grief will come, you'll go back to being fully 'in your body' when the presentation is done, and you'll keep up with your tedious chores while thinking of more exciting things.

Dysphoria and Dissociation

Dysphoria seems to be strongly linked with depersonalization (the feeling that you're not connected to yourself) and derealization (the feeling that you're not connected to the world) (Jones 2017). This makes perfect sense when you recognize that dysphoria is a long-lasting and often overwhelming source of trauma for many trans and/or non-binary people. There are also many similarities between the feelings (or lack thereof) associated with all three experiences, with a sense of detachment from the self, a feeling that your internal felt sense doesn't fit well with reality, and a general feeling that something is 'wrong'.

The severity or unpleasantness of dissociation seems to reduce when trans people are able to access appropriate medical transition, which often lessens dysphoria (Colizzi *et al.* 2015). I know from personal experience and from talking to my therapy clients that working compassionately to lessen your own dysphoria and become more in line with who you feel you are can help you to feel more connected to yourself and the world in general. For me, alleviating my main sources of dysphoria gave me the emotional space and energy to reconnect with myself in general, which was a big factor in dealing with my own depersonalization. My clients have also described this process, and many have described how becoming more in touch with what they need to be less dysphoric has opened doors for them to address other needs and find new ways to care for themselves that they hadn't been able to think of before. Clients whose dysphoria and trans identity was something that they had been dissociating away have described coming to terms with being trans as 'feeling emotions like never before', 'being more in touch with life', 'understanding so much more' about themselves, and 'the colours coming back in to the world'.

The Person-Centred Theory of the Dialogical Self

According to the person-centred theory of the dialogical self, everybody has several configurations of self. These configurations are several separate parts of your personality that form one whole, coherent 'self' (Mearns and Thorne 2000). Essentially, the theory posits that your whole self is made up of several selves, which are different configurations of the self that have split off to deal with different experiences (Cooper *et al.* 2004).

Over the course of a lifetime, we develop several personalities that we use in different circumstances. For some of us, those aspects of ourselves won't be very different, but for others they can become something very unlike how we experience our definition of our 'self'. Even if you feel like there's only one of you within yourself, you may experience inner configurations of yourself that align with the idea of an inner child, the professional persona you have to be at work, or your inner critic (like the 'critical inner voice' mentioned in the *Depression* chapter of this book). You may be able to switch between these different selves at will if you find yourself putting on a lot of different hats in life, for example being 'professional you' at work and then 'parent you' as soon as you get home. In some people, these different versions of the self can be so different from the whole self and from each other that they become like different people in one body, leading to dissociative identities. These identities may be known as personalities, alters, others, or multiples.

When Dissociating Affects You Negatively

As normal as dissociating is, if you find yourself dissociating often or intensely it can be frightening, disorienting, frustrating, and unhelpful. For example, if you find yourself losing time, feeling strong emotions that don't feel like they're 'yours', not feeling any emotions at all, or experiencing yourself as very removed from what's going on around you for an extended period of time, this can be exceedingly confusing and scary.

You might also experience plurality, which is the experience of being one of two or more people who all experience their thoughts and feelings in the same body. Some people describe this as being part of a 'system' of personalities or voices. This is not always a negative issue – some people who are part of a system can live comfortably with their alters, including sharing co-consciousness and working as a team to live healthy and happy lives. For others, the problem comes when some of these dissociative personalities are malevolent, when not everybody in the system understands that they are part of a system, when a personality who is not equipped or designed for a situation is forced into one, when amnesic barriers are experienced, or when one or more of these alters become confused, frightened, or angry regarding their existence as part of the system.

A few of these ideas have been mentioned in other chapters but they can be very useful for grounding yourself in your here and now, and I think they're worth mentioning again. Others are fresh and new, just for you.

- *Check-in times.* Check in with yourself as often as you can through the day. How are you feeling? Do you have any physical needs that you need to be aware of right now? Are you feeling safe? What do you need right now?

- *Dysphoria and euphoria check-ins.* Pay gentle, curious attention to your experience of gender dysphoria and euphoria as you go about your day. Is anything about your current circumstances making you feel closer to, or further away from, your body and your experience of yourself? Are there any changes you can make to these circumstances right now that might help you to feel connected to who you really are?

- *Make a safe space.* Create a physical space that makes you feel safe, with objects and features that make you feel grounded in the here and now. Surround yourself with textures that you like, sounds that make you feel safe, and some of your current favourite things.

- *Move.* Moving in ways that feel good can help you to feel grounded in, and connected to, your body. You might start with some simple stretching or walking as your body allows and noticing the different ways your body moves and feels as you do different things.

- *Create a journal.* You can do this by writing, drawing, or making videos, or in any way that speaks to you. Keep a journal of how you are feeling and what you are thinking every day (or as often as you remember). This can help you to process your emotions and become more grounded, but can also serve as a record of what you've been up to if you experience loss of time or dissociative 'blackouts'. If you are part of a system, you can also use this journal together as a way to communicate how you are all feeling and process this together.

- *The 5-4-3-2-1 exercise.* Get yourself comfortable, take a breath, and then find five things you can see, four things you can hear, three things you can touch, two things you can smell, and one thing you can taste. Try to remain grounded in one spot for the exercise, but it's okay to get up and move around to find these things, especially if you don't have anything to smell or taste at hand.

- *Safety breathing.* Notice how you are breathing right now. Take a breath in for the count of four. At the top of the breath, say out loud or in your head, 'I am safe.' Exhale for the count of four. At the bottom of the breath, repeat, 'I am safe.' Do this for as long as you like, and then notice how your breathing has changed. It can help to put a hand on your chest if this doesn't give you dysphoria; otherwise, you can put a hand on your tummy or feel your breath in your nose or mouth.

- *Grounding objects.* Think about an object you own that you really like. Hold it in your hand and notice how it feels. Is it smooth or rough? Hard or soft? Cold or hot? Does it feel different in different areas or in different parts of your hand? Keep this object with you for times when you're dissociating, and hold it comfortably to remind you of where you are.

Different Identities of Different Genders

If you find yourself dissociating in a way that means you are part of a plural system of alters, some of those personalities may not be the same gender as you. They may be the gender you were assigned at birth, which might cause you some distress and dysphoria. It is also worth stating that being part of a system where other personalities are your assigned gender at birth does not mean you are not trans – if you are not the gender you were assigned at birth, you can still identify as trans even if other parts of your system don't feel that way about themselves. If you have the experience of having different aspects of your self, and some of those configurations of personality have genders that are different to yours, this does not mean that you are not your gender.

You might also find that the genders of your alters may change or that alters of different genders become more present in your system as you explore your gender, especially if you choose to take HRT (Mun *et al.* 2020). You might also find yourself becoming more co-conscious, or experiencing some synthesis, with other alters of different genders. It can be a confusing time when the make-up of your system changes and it may take a lot of processing, but your experience of your gender is still yours and yours alone.

Loving Life as a Trans System (Or Not)

Some people find real joy and community in being part of an internal system of different people. Plurality can be seen as a gift and as a way to talk directly to different parts of yourself and meet your complicated, differing needs in a more direct way. Together, you can explore how you feel in different situations, share new ideas, and play around with gender and presentation. Clients I've spoken to who are part of systems have told me that they always have someone to talk to and bounce ideas off, and that they can use the multiple ways of experiencing the same event to gain further insights into what has happened to them. Working well together as a system means working hard to communicate to your selves and to other people, as well as keeping your selves safe. You will all have different needs to meet and different ideas on how to meet those needs, and these differences should be acknowledged and cherished as you work together to get what you need.

For others, things may be much less comfortable. You may wish to integrate or 'quieten' the other identities that exist with you, especially if some of these alters have a negative impact on your life. For some people, letting their alters be heard and understood can lead to a synthesis, assimilation, or integration of these alters (when alters become a more unified part of the whole self or become a new merged personality with one or more other alters). This can be preferable but often involves a high level of understanding and empathy for parts of yourself that you'd rather not look at and letting parts of yourself that you don't like 'front' or be more conscious of what's happening, which can be an uncomfortable experience.

Ultimately, the choice of whether or not you enjoy being part of a system, wish to integrate into a whole self, or somewhere in between is down to you and your system. Either way, talking to a knowledgeable mental health practitioner about what you're going through can be an excellent way to get what you need.

Answering Intrusive Thoughts

Intrusive thoughts are usually incongruent, sudden, and intense. That means it can feel like there's something in you that inputs things you don't believe and don't want to think into your head, accompanied by a physical urge to act on them and an emotional confusion or revulsion at the thought. This can range from the ominous and violent ('Use that knife to hurt yourself'), to the sacrilegious (an urge to scream while in a place of worship), to the bizarre ('Throw your glasses off the bridge'), to the embarrassing ('Take a bite out of that person's sandwich'), to the morbid (an image of driving into a wall while in your car), to the sexual (an image of an unwanted sex act), to the seemingly benign but unwelcomely repetitive (I once had the chorus to Rocket Man by Elton John stuck in my head for a full year, despite multiple attempts to remove it and fully against my wishes. I laugh at this now but it was incredibly distressing at the time!) (Ryan 2018). They may also take the form of unwanted memories and flashbacks, which can appear as images, thoughts, sounds, emotions, and more.

Intrusive thoughts tend to be a product of your inner self processing things that you don't like or that you feel anxious about (Hirsch and Holmes 2007) and dealing with them in a dissociated way (Reese 2011). For example, internal worries like 'What if I hurt my partner?' and 'I'm frightened that my partner will die' can emerge as a sudden and inexplicable urge to smother your partner with a pillow, which you'll probably and understandably react to with horror. These thoughts can manifest as images, words, physical urges, or a combination of these phenomena.

These thoughts are distressing, but they're perfectly normal. You're not wrong or bad for having them – this is just another (kind of weird) way that your brain is trying to keep you safe. The fact that these thoughts are intrusive means you don't actually want them to happen – they're incongruent by nature, which means they don't follow your moral code. If you're having intrusive thoughts about bad things happening, it's probably because you're actually a good person!

A key to working through your intrusive thoughts is to remind yourself that you're safe. Answer the thought with a complementary thought, whether that's in words, images, or an intentional urge. If your intrusive thought was an image of throwing your hot coffee in someone's face, for example, recognize that you're worried about how your hot coffee might hurt someone, and try to visualize smiling at someone while holding your coffee tightly in your hand. You might even like to acknowledge and thank your intrusive thought for making you aware of a worry that you might otherwise have missed.

Feeling Numb, Empty, or Far Away

If you find yourself dissociating in any way, you may find yourself feeling hollow, numb, or far away from the world. As your inner processes work to keep you safe by dissociating different memories, emotions, and parts of you, this can affect your capacity to access your emotions and sense of self in a wider sense, causing you to feel like your emotions and identity have been stripped from you or squashed away somewhere that you can't reach. This can last for a short time or for a very long time.

Something that can help to lessen this experience is reminding yourself as often as you can that any emotions you do feel are welcome and healthy. Chances are, one or more of your emotions are being dissociated in order to keep you safe, so be prepared for uncomfortable emotions such as anger and grief to come up. Remember that these feelings are there to offer you helpful information and that you can experience them and work with them to grow through them. As you start to feel emotions more fully or more often, try to greet these emotions with compassionate curiosity and start to experiment with how you might want to express these emotions. A good start might be simply announcing your feelings to yourself out loud and seeing how that feels, which sounds kind of cheesy but might help you to process what's actually happening with you.

Tuning in to your felt sense of your body can also be very helpful in this situation. While you may be feeling emotionally numb right now, your body may still be responding to your feelings. You might want to check in with yourself often and be still with your body, paying attention to your physical feelings. Does your body feel tense or relaxed? How is your breathing right now? How hard is your heart beating? Do any particular parts of you feel different than usual? These might be clues that you can look at gently to determine how you're feeling right now and what you might need to do to meet your needs. You can do this pretty casually by just listening to your body for a minute or so and seeing what happens, or you can take part in a body-scan exercise that spends time bringing awareness to each of your specific body parts. The aim here is to notice what's happening in your body, not to struggle against that feeling or to worry about it – just to notice what is happening, build up a picture of what you might be feeling right now, and keep breathing. This way of knowing yourself can help you to connect to your feelings again.

Body Scan

If you'd like to be more connected to how you feel in your body right now, you can complete something called a body scan. This is a way to connect with different body parts one by one, noticing how they feel and relaxing them in turn.

Find a comfortable, quiet, and private place to rest. Most people like to lie on their back somewhere comfortable, but however is most comfortable to you is just fine. If you're cold, you can get comfy with some blankets, and you might want to use pillows for your head and under your knees for some extra support.

To start, close your eyes, or let your gaze unfocus if that doesn't feel comfortable. Be with your breath for a while and notice how quickly and how deeply you're breathing. Take note of how your whole body feels right now in general. Notice if you are experiencing any pain, discomfort, or muscle tightness, and notice where your body touches the floor or any other surfaces.

Start at the top of your body and work down. Working through this list as slowly as possible, pay attention to the physical feelings in these body parts, recognize them, and then aim to relax these body parts as much as you can: forehead, eyes, jaw, neck, left shoulder, left arm, left elbow, left wrist, left hand, the fingers on your left hand, right shoulder, right arm, right elbow, right wrist, right hand, the fingers on your right hand, chest, tummy, upper back, lower back, bottom, left thigh, left knee, left calf and shin, left ankle, left foot, the toes on your left foot, right thigh, right knee, right calf and shin, right ankle, right foot, and the toes on your right foot.

Return to your breathing and to your awareness of your body as a whole. Pay attention to the physical feelings in your body and recognize them. From here, you can either rest for a while longer or open your eyes and start to move around slowly and gently. You can spend a little time reflecting on your experience and how you felt before, during, and after the body scan. Did you notice that some parts were particularly uncomfortable today? Did you find it difficult or easy to relax your body? Were you able to concentrate through the body scan, or did your attention drift at any points? Do you feel more or less grounded after the exercise than you did at the beginning?

You can do this body scan at any time that suits you, but it's particularly useful in helping you to feel gently grounded in your body, for example during a period of dissociation, and it can be a soothing thing to do before going to bed after a day that's made you feel cognitively frazzled.

Making It Through Periods of Depersonalization

If you find yourself feeling disconnected from your body and your feelings for a short period of time after an acute trauma, such as experiencing an emotional shock or being involved in an accident, you might find yourself feeling numb or like your body is moving without direction from your thoughts. Try to remember that this is your mind protecting you from pain. It may feel uncomfortable or scary but the experience will not last forever. It may help to try to come back to your body in small and gentle ways. Eating strong mints, listening to loud music, drinking a hot or very cold drink (while trying to make sure it's not hot or cold enough to damage you), and seeking out enjoyable physical pressure, like a short massage or lying under a weighted blanket, might help. Actively resting may also help, which might include paying attention to your breathing, being touched by a loved one, watching a treasured film, having a gentle conversation with a loved one, or setting up a fort or nest somewhere safe. You may think these may seem like simple things and you'd be right – these activities are unlikely to stop you from being completely depersonalized. The aim is to try to 'come back to yourself' gently and compassionately, because overstimulating yourself or trying to bump back down to your body might be re-traumatizing.

Prolonged periods of depersonalization usually arise from extended periods of depression and trauma; again, because your mind wants to protect you from further pain. Focusing on your emotional and physical safety, and on your daily self-care needs, can make a big difference over time. Hold on to the parts of yourself, your relationships, and your life that you feel some connection to and work outwards from there. Talking about current life events with trusted loved ones who make you feel safe can eventually help this numbness to fade away. Having repeated check-in sessions with yourself, where you notice your breathing and how your body feels, can help you to feel more connected to yourself again, as can scheduling regular time to have somebody touch you in a way that you find grounding, like getting a hug from a loved one or a massage from a physiotherapist. Talking to a counsellor or therapist, especially a trauma-focused expert, can also be extremely helpful.

Making It Through Periods of Derealization

After an acute trauma, like being in an accident or having a panic attack, you might experience the things around you as being washed out and colourless, and you might feel like you can't connect to what's happening around you. When people talk to you they might sound far away, and you might feel spaced out or foggy, like you're moving through a dream. Being around trusted loved ones can help you to feel connected to the world again through them, and engaging in activities with loved ones in which you connect both to them and the outside world can be particularly helpful. This might involve listening to podcasts or watching TV shows that have hosts or characters you feel connected to, being outside with friends, holding a grounding object, being somewhere calm in nature, and spending time with pets.

If you find yourself experiencing derealization chronically, remember that this is your brain trying to keep you safe from further harm by making potentially harmful things seem further away from you. Anything that can remind you that you are safe and that you can deal with the highs and lows of real life can be really helpful. Take some time to do the kind of self-care that helps you to feel capable, strong, and resilient, whatever that looks like for you. Talking to trusted loved ones and therapists who are experts in trauma can be incredibly helpful in understanding how you're feeling and re-understanding the world.

The Aftermath of Dissociation

After you've experienced some kind of dissociation, you're likely to experience a mix of thoughts, feelings, and inner situations.

You may find that you're experiencing some memory loss after dissociating, and you might feel disoriented or confused. Using grounding exercises, like the ones mentioned in this chapter, can be an excellent way of coming back to yourself and to your body. Alternatively, you may also experience a flood of memories and flashbacks to the time when you dissociated. You might find yourself overwhelmed with emotions, too, especially if you experienced depersonalization and a resulting lack of felt emotions. While this may be distressing, it's important to experience those memories and feel those emotions as they come to you and not dissociate them further. It might be helpful to contact someone you trust so you can talk them through what has happened to you and what you're feeling, and ask them if they can fill in any blanks in your memory. Many of my clients report feeling exhausted after a period of dissociation, as well as needing an extended period of physical and emotional recovery, which can look like talking with a mental health professional, attending diligently to self-care needs, and resting as much as possible. Ultimately, you're likely to be feeling a little emotionally tender after dissociating, so whatever self-care you find most helpful is going to be beneficial and well deserved.

For When You Can't Go On

In this chapter, we'll explore how suicidal ideation and mental health crisis situations might look and feel, how to keep yourself safe in a crisis, what you can do if someone you know is in crisis, and some reminders of why your life is worth living.

Before You Read This Chapter

Discussing thoughts and emotions around suicide can bring up intense feelings in many people, so please remember to take breaks while reading this chapter if you need to. It might help to read this in a place that you can make as safe as possible – maybe a blanket nest in your bedroom with your headphones on or in a trusted wide-open space where you can feel the breeze, whatever makes you feel grounded and calm. It might also help to plan a 'decompression' activity for afterwards, such as writing in a journal, speaking to a friend, or having a warm bath. If you feel like you need more support or someone to talk to, you can find extra resources in the *Charities, Helplines, and Other Free Advice* chapter of this book.

What Is Suicidal Ideation?

If you feel like you can't go on, you're likely experiencing suicidal ideation. This means that you've been thinking, in some capacity, about ending your life (American Psychiatric Association 2013). These can be fleeting and rare thoughts for you, or these thoughts might be with you constantly over a long period of time. Many people experience something in between. Thoughts can range in severity from thinking passively about suicide to actively planning to end your life (Klonsky, May, and Saffer 2016).

If you find yourself thinking about ending things, this is a sure sign that you need some extra support in life as soon as possible. You may be feeling suicidal because you feel depressed, anxious, hopeless, trapped, exhausted, or worthless, or for many other reasons. As a trans person, you may also be dealing with many traumatic feelings and events that feel inescapable, such as dysphoria, social exclusion, and shame. You may also find it hard to talk about your problems, and you may feel that you're unable to cope because of how different or alone you believe you are (McDermot, Hughes, and Rawlings 2018). Almost half of trans people have reported that they have attempted suicide at some point in their lives, with 84% reporting that they've thought about it (FRA 2012; Nottinghamshire Healthcare NHS Foundation Trust 2017; PACE 2015).

Suicidal ideation is fairly common and nothing to be ashamed of. This does not mean you are 'going mad' or that you are a bad person; you may just need more help than you are currently receiving.

Passive and Active Ideation

When you're feeling suicidal, this can be experienced actively and passively (Beck, Kovacs, and Weissman 1979). If you are experiencing passive suicide ideation, you may not want to be alive or you may spend time thinking about what life would look like if you weren't in it. This might look like thoughts such as, 'The world would be better off without me,' 'I don't deserve to be alive,' 'I wish I wasn't here,' 'I don't think I can do this any more,' or 'I wish I was dead.' More active suicide ideation might mean you are considering taking your own life or making plans to do so. Active suicide ideation may involve planning the method you would use to attempt suicide, preparing how you would say goodbye to loved ones, and gathering the means to take your own life.

You might experience more passive or more active ideation at the same time in your life. For example, you may be experiencing passively suicidal thoughts frequently for a while and then experience more active suicidal ideation after a specific event, or you may have tackled a period of very active suicidal ideation and feel like you are doing much better, but still be thinking passively suicidal thoughts afterwards.

When Your Emotions Are in Crisis

You may feel particularly suicidal when you're in a crisis – that is, when you feel completely overwhelmed by emotion, or when you feel nothing at all due to intense dissociation. You might be having panic attacks, experiencing intense flashbacks, self-harming, feeling manic or incredibly low, feeling uncontrollably angry, believing things you know aren't true, or seeing and hearing things that aren't there. You're likely to feel out of control, overwhelmed, and like you might hurt yourself.

These emotions and thoughts can be so intense that you barely feel like yourself, never mind remembering how to do grounding exercises, so it can be incredibly difficult to utilize any good mental health skills that might otherwise be helpful. Self-care techniques that usually help you might be completely forgotten as your ability to think clearly changes, or useful self-care techniques may stop working for you altogether in a time of crisis. This is absolutely not your fault, although it may feel like it – it just means you need something else, now.

The first important thing to do when you are in crisis is to make sure you are as physically safe as possible. Your emotional and physical safety is paramount, now more than ever, and it is the first thing you'll need to think about. Even if you do not intend to hurt yourself, it can be much easier to injure yourself or make yourself ill through disorientation or neglect when you're in crisis. Can you keep yourself safe? Can anyone else help to keep you safe right now? This might involve contacting people you trust and asking for practical support, and making sure the area you're in is safe from potentially dangerous items including weapons, medications, heavy or sharp objects, and ligatures like rope. You may not feel like having company right now, but having somebody come over or going to a loved one's place might be your safest option. You may also need some help to care for yourself in other ways, so having someone you trust prompt you to drink and rest can be extremely helpful.

The kind of support you need to stay safe may include having someone you trust to talk to, such as a friend, your therapist, or a helpline, such as the Switchboard LGBT+ Helpline or the National Trans 24hr Helpline in the UK or Trans Lifeline in the US (you can find the details for these services and many more in the *Charities, Helplines, and Other Free Advice* chapter of this book). Having someone hear your story and offer empathy can be a powerful way to express your emotions, feel safe, and become more grounded in the moment.

You may also find that you need different kinds of support from different sources. It's okay to reach out to multiple sources for help. It may feel shameful or embarrassing that people know you're vulnerable right now, but it can help you to get what you need and can help you feel safer in the long run. In my experience, people want to help! For example, you might ask one trusted person to come over and keep you safe while you speak to your therapist on the phone, another to let you stay at their house for the evening to make sure you're not alone, and another to help you schedule a doctor's appointment so you can receive some medical help.

If you feel that you cannot keep yourself safe while going through this crisis, it is important to take care of yourself by getting immediate help. This might look like making an emergency appointment with your doctor, calling your local crisis team, calling 111 in the UK, or calling an ambulance at 999 (UK) or 911 (US).

When you feel yourself coming out of a crisis situation, you are likely to feel emotionally and physically exhausted. Taking care of yourself now is likely to look like keeping yourself as safe as possible while resting and nourishing your body and beginning to process your crisis. You may want to keep expressing your emotions to those you trust while also taking part in soothing activities that allow you to recover, like listening to gentle audiobooks in bed or going for an easy stroll with a friend.

If It Keeps You Here, It's Worth It

In the *Self-Care* chapter of this book, there's a section prompting you to consider whether your self-care techniques are harmful as well as helpful. If you are in crisis or ready to take your own life, any self-care technique you have that helps is worth trying, even if it's a little more harmful than you would otherwise like (Davies *et al.* 2020; Shaw 2012). Of course, this is not me encouraging you to hurt yourself in any lasting or extreme way. This is more of an acknowledgement that your self-care options that might also be a little bit bad for you might be worth a try if you're in extreme distress. If you find yourself in a crisis and healthy coping mechanisms aren't working for you, there are worse things than having a couple of cigarettes to calm down if you know it will help just for today, for example. When you're feeling better, try to give yourself a break about this and return to your self-care techniques that don't involve any harm.

While more 'extreme' self-care techniques might be helpful right now, this also applies the other way. You may find that the very basics of self-care are what's keeping you going right now, and that's alright. When you're feeling like you can't go on, investing in your continued survival by trying to eat well, stay hydrated, sleep soundly, and stay safe can be very powerful. It's also okay if what's getting you through a crisis is that you have to hang around long enough to see the new series of your favourite TV programme or that your cat would be sad if you're gone. These are the basic building blocks of our lives and there is no shame in them being important to you.

Preparing for a Future Crisis

There's always a possibility that you may be in emotional crisis in the future, especially if you're experiencing poor mental health or ongoing trauma right now. Creating a crisis plan and putting it somewhere easy to see can be an excellent way to feel safer sooner when you're next feeling overwhelmed or like you may harm yourself. This plan can include helplines and other services that you know you can call in an emergency, the numbers of important people like your therapist and your support network, as well as any self-care you can do that often works well for you when you feel that you're approaching crisis point. A few clients have found this information particularly easy to process in the form of a flowchart. If you're in the UK, you can also download the Stay Alive app, which can help you to make a safety plan that you can access through mobile devices.

Asking trusted people in advance to see how they might be able to help in the future can be really helpful for you, as you will be more aware of what support is available to you when you're in crisis, and also really helpful for your support network, who can set needed boundaries and prepare themselves. You might also be able to advise them on any signs to look out for that show you're approaching a crisis point. For example, if you know that you tend to withdraw from loved ones as you get closer to a crisis, you can organize for friends to contact you and check that you're okay if they haven't heard from you within a certain amount of time.

Remember Your Future Euphoria

Somewhere, sometime, in the future, there is a you that made it through this. There's a you that's not in crisis and is not suicidal, who has found a way through this and has moved on to new things. There is a you in the future who feels happy and calm – not all of the time, but sometimes, or maybe a lot of the time when their life is going particularly smoothly. There is future-you who has survived.

I know that you probably don't believe me when I say that

it gets better, because I didn't believe that either when I was at crisis point. When people said that to me I would think, *Well yeah, that worked for you, but it won't work for me.* But, with lots of change, lots of hard work, and lots of support, it did get better for me. I've seen my clients, my colleagues, and my loved ones feel better, too. I've seen myself and so many others survive – not only that, but start to thrive.

It might be difficult to picture right now, because it's difficult to imagine or remember positive experiences when you're feeling rough (Joorman, Siemer, and Gotlib 2007; Romero, Sanchez, and Vazquez 2014), but it can be helpful to try to imagine a life beyond where you are now. Try to imagine the circumstances in which you are a little happier, and follow that image wherever you need to go.

This also applies to your transition, whatever form that might take going forward. If you can imagine yourself just a little bit happier in your gender presentation, or a little more confident in who you are, or a little less gender dysphoric and a little more gender euphoric, what does that look like for you? Hold the image gently and let it tell you what next right thing you might need to do. It's been found (Bauer *et al.* 2015) that the suicide risk for trans people lowers significantly as they access wanted medical transition services, socially transition in ways they want to, and face less prejudice from those around them – so, whatever will help you to feel comfortable as a trans person is likely to help you overall. Your gender euphoria will be there for you if you hold on.

Crisis Care for Others

If someone you love is in an emotional crisis, here are a few tips that you can use that could help. There's a focus on helping a loved one, here, but you can apply these same tips to yourself if you find yourself in crisis, too.

You can help to schedule a doctor's appointment and try to make sure your loved one attends. If this appointment takes place by phone, maybe you can make sure you're around that day as practical and emotional support. If the appointment takes place in your loved one's doctor's practice, you should be able to chaperone them and accompany them in the appointment if you say it's needed.

You can talk with your loved one about setting up different plans for different emotions and states of being. They might need a different kind of company when they're sad than when they're angry, for example, or they might need different tools to take care of themselves depending on how intense their emotions are. You can help to set up these plans in advance, so you and your loved one feel safe and knowledgeable about what is needed in different circumstances. You can also discuss what to do if self-harm behaviours become severe, for example if your loved one has hurt themselves gravely enough to need medical attention – is there a medical professional they would prefer to contact? Having a plan could help to take the pressure off you having to do all kinds of caring at once and the pressure off your loved one in terms of knowing they can have the types of help they need.

Try to make sure there are other people that your loved one can call. I know this might be difficult in many ways, but getting other people involved for different care needs could be really helpful – it means some of the pressure is off you, and your loved one gets their needs met by safe people. For example, maybe you can agree to chat with your loved one once a day until they feel their crisis has passed, while another person can agree to be there to help your loved one cook, and a professional can agree to be on standby in case the crisis becomes more severe, etc. If you're in the UK, you or your loved one can call the Switchboard LGBT+ Helpline for more help, and you and/or your loved one can call, text, or email this service to speak to an LGBTQ+ person who's there to talk to about anything at any time, including during a crisis. I've heard really good things about the service from lots of different people. You can find their number in the *Charities, Helplines, and Other Free Advice* chapter of this book. In an emergency, there's also your local crisis team (if you're in the UK, you can find their number on the NHS website), the emergency services, and A&E. Accessing these services can be really helpful or really rough – sometimes both. It can be necessary to access one or all of these services if your loved one is making plans or taking steps to end their life, if they have injuries after self-harming, if they are hurt to the point of confusion or unconsciousness, or if you think they're unable to cope at home right now.

Try not to use blaming or shaming language about what is happening to, or in front of, the person who is in crisis. This won't help and it's not their fault. If you're feeling overwhelmed, it's okay to negotiate what you can do for the person at this time, and it's okay to take a break.

While you're caring for someone who's going through a crisis, it's important to avoid your own mental health crisis by making sure you're caring for yourself as well as possible right now. Try to focus on making sure you're eating, hydrated, resting, sleeping, washing, and attending to any other self-care needs. Remember that your needs are important, too, and that you deserve to care for yourself.

A Trans Life Is Worth Living

Please remember that a trans life is worth living. So many of us go on to have fulfilling and beautiful lives in which we are loved and appreciated. Being who you are in the face of oppression can be horrific, but if you stay true to yourself, you can live as *you*, and you are really, genuinely, effortlessly awesome. There is so much that you are capable of as a trans person, and everything you can do matters. You have a future ahead of you that is worth hanging on to, even if it's hard to imagine – trans people can and do thrive and grow old, and you can be one of them.

You will not always feel like this. That is a promise. A crisis experience will not, and cannot, last forever. How you're feeling right now isn't weakness, and neither is asking for help. Even if you feel you're at absolute rock bottom, even if it feels like nothing will ever be alright again, this is not a weak time in your life, this is not a failure, and there is help out there including and beyond this book.

If in doubt, please check in with your doctor and tell them what's going on. Call your local crisis helpline and talk to someone. See if you can find accessible therapy. Call your loved ones and let them know you need a hand. Please, please try to hold on. Your community is here to laugh with you, cry with you, nap with you, and watch weird cartoons with you. That includes me, too – I'm with you in spirit through these pages, and I promise I'm not the only one. Things might be incredibly bad, but I know how strong you've had to be to survive at all. Together, we can keep going.

There's Help Out There

In this chapter we'll explore issues like what to expect if you ask your doctor for more mental health support, what it's like to be on anti-depressants, how to find a therapist who can help you, and some of the different kinds of community support available.

It's Okay to Ask for Help

Everyone needs extra support sometimes and it's okay to ask for what you need. You deserve all of the help that you need and more, and there's no shame in needing a little support or a lot. Professionals who are trained to look after your mental health are also trained not to judge you for any help that you ask for, and almost all of them will be happy to offer all the support that they can. You shouldn't need to worry that a professional helper will be mad at you or think less of you for seeking support, or that you don't deserve to take up a professional's time – in fact, for many mental health professionals (including me!), learning about people's needs so they can help to meet them is a well-loved vocation, something that we're excited and passionate about. We love to help, so we love it when you ask!

In this chapter, we'll specifically be looking at asking medical professionals, mental health practitioners, and peer support groups for help, but please don't forget that it's also okay to ask other people in life for help, too. Although loved ones, colleagues, tutors, and other people in your community may not be able to offer medicine or therapy, they may be able to help you to meet other needs by providing emotional support or practical help.

Seeing Your Doctor about Your Mental Health

If you decide to see your doctor about your mental health, there's a high chance you can be seen relatively quickly in the UK. You may feel very nervous about going to see your doctor, but please remember that they are paid to listen to your symptoms and to act accordingly. Nobody at your medical practice (or in general) should treat you like you are bad or wrong for what you tell your doctor. Your doctor is there to help you, and you will not be the first or last person to speak to them about any of the things you're going through. If your doctor does not offer you any treatment, or if they treat you poorly during your appointment, it is fully within your rights to complain and to ask to see another doctor. Your mental health should always be taken seriously.

Most likely, if you let your doctor know that you've been struggling with your mental health, your doctor will offer you short-term, NHS-funded therapy that is likely to be based in either mindfulness or Cognitive Behavioural Therapy (CBT). The waiting list for these services tends to be quite long, and you can expect to wait anywhere from a few months to over a year.

You may also be offered a short-term, low-dose course of 'starter' medicine, usually an SSRI (selective serotonin reuptake inhibitor – a category of anti-depressants), such as citalopram, fluoxetine, or sertraline, or a beta blocker (which helps with the physical symptoms of anxiety), such as propranolol. You will be asked to make a check-up appointment with your doctor for about a month later to discuss how any treatment is progressing and to talk through your next steps. These next steps might include increasing your dose of medication, changing the medication you're on, adding in another type of medication, chasing up with mental health services and referrals, and stopping your medication.

It may also be worth asking your doctor if they can sign-post you to any groups or meet-ups for people with your issues or symptoms. These groups can be incredibly useful in helping you find community and peer-led mental health resources. This may be particularly useful if there is a long waiting list for NHS-funded therapy.

It is up to you if you feel happy to try any of the options you are offered by your doctor. If there's anything you feel uncomfortable with, you're always allowed to ask for more information and more time, or to ask for a different kind of treatment. Your care is your choice!

Dealing with Trans Broken Arm Syndrome

You may have to advocate for yourself more than cis people would when you seek out mental health care. This is due to a specific kind of transphobia and cissexism that is unfortunately common in healthcare, known as Trans Broken Arm Syndrome (Payton 2015; Knutson et al. 2017). This is when, for example, a transfeminine person breaks their arm after an accident and tries to get medical help from A&E, only to be told by a doctor that the broken arm has actually been caused by the oestrogen they take and that they need to stop HRT. Even with a clear cause, healthcare providers have a habit of blaming all medical issues on being transgender.

Self-advocating for your mental health can be as scary as it is necessary. Try to remember that healthcare providers are there to work for you, and try to be calm and persistent about the care you need. You can bring notes about your symptoms and how you've been feeling if you find yourself forgetting things due to nerves. If you feel that you're being met with Trans Broken Arm Syndrome, take a deep breath and ask, 'What would you say about these symptoms if you were talking to a cisgender person?'

Sticking with competent and trustworthy healthcare providers, if you can, can also be a helpful way to get good mental healthcare. If there is a mental health practitioner, a doctor, or someone else involved in your care that you trust, don't be afraid to ask specifically for their services the next time you need to see someone. Healthcare providers that you trust will take you seriously as a trans and/or non-binary person can also be helpful sources of referrals to other care, for example a helpful doctor who has had trans-inclusive training may know a therapist in the area who has also had trans-inclusive training. With this in mind, other trans people in your community can also be a great source of knowledge about which healthcare practitioners are trans-friendly in your area.

You can and should make use of your right to a chaperone in many healthcare settings, and it may be helpful to enlist someone you trust who is cisgender to come with you and advocate on your behalf. While it's shocking that this is still needed, it's definitely been my experience that bringing someone with more obvious privilege than you to a healthcare appointment can negate many of the effects of transphobia and oppression that can be found in medical settings.

It's also important that you let your mental healthcare providers know about any transition-related medication you're on if they ask, even if it might be tempting not to. Although there's a risk that you may face Trans Broken Arm Syndrome, it's also important for some healthcare providers to know exactly what medication you're taking and what other treatments you're having so that they can practise safely and avoid giving you treatment or advice that might react badly with your medication.

Considering Anti-Depressants

If you're experiencing symptoms of depression, post-traumatic stress, distressing dissociation, or anxiety, it might be worth looking into what anti-depressant medications are available for you. You won't be alone – around three quarters of trans people report having taken anti-depressants (McNeil *et al.* 2012). For most people most of the time, it's very safe to take anti-depressants while also taking HRT.

Many people expect their anti-depressants to make them feel happier and, while this is the case for some people, they don't work that way for others. Anti-depressants don't function as 'uppers', so the right dose and type of anti-depressants for you are more likely to make you feel less numb and more clear-headed so that you then have the energy to engage in the self-care, therapy, hobbies, relational work, life changes, and other steps that will help you feel happier. Taking anti-depressants is like getting an extra leg-up as you try to find your way to an upwards spiral of good mental health.

Deciding whether or not to take anti-depressants can be a really difficult decision to make. Like many other kinds of medications, different types of anti-depressants will have different effects and side effects, and they can be a mixed bag until you find one that works for you. With these downsides in mind, anti-depressants can also be exceedingly helpful and they may even save your life.

You will need to have access to a doctor that you don't mind sharing your symptoms with in order to get anti-depressants. If you and your doctor decide you could benefit from trying anti-depressants, you'll most likely be given a low 'starter' dose and told to make another appointment to discuss how you're doing. If you're managing the side effects well and things seem to be improving a little for you, chances are you're all set, but it's important to monitor your feelings, thoughts, and side effects to make sure things continue to go well for you. You'll need to take most kinds of anti-depressants for at least six months before you consider coming off them. After that time period, and with the help of your doctor, it's totally up to you how long you take your anti-depressants for. So long as they're useful to you, it's okay to keep taking them. It's also worth taking them for a little while after you feel better so that you can keep working to make sure that will stay the same after you've stopped taking your medication. If, after six months, they stop being useful or start feeling harmful, it's okay to stop them, with advice from your doctor. It can sometimes be scary to think about your life without the anti-depressants that may have helped you, so it's important to have as strong a support network as you can around you, including your mental health team, while you stop taking your anti-depressants.

It's also usually an option to change the anti-depressants you are taking if you feel that anti-depressants may still be helpful but the ones you're taking aren't agreeing with you. The wrong type or dose of anti-depressants can make you feel fuzzy-headed or like your emotions have been blunted, in which case it can be useful to try a different kind of anti-depressant or a lower dose. Other medications that aren't anti-depressants, like beta blockers, may also be helpful. Medications aren't perfect and some won't be perfect for you, but others can be an excellent fit. It might be frightening when you reach out for help and get medication that makes you feel no different, or even poorly if you have initial side effects, but there are other types of help and other types of medications to try. It's okay to keep trying to find the right treatment for you.

It's also worth remembering that other people may try to make you feel like taking anti-depressants makes you weak. These people are wrong – seeking help, and following through with the things that help, makes you strong.

Finding a Therapist

If you do not want to wait to see an NHS therapist or counsellor, and you want to avoid the waiting lists for free counselling that are common in the UK under the NHS, there are many private therapists you can contact. While you are looking for a private counsellor, psychotherapist, or another type of private mental health worker, there are many factors to consider.

Depending on the area you live in, and the type of therapy you'd like to receive, one hour-long therapy session in the UK can cost between about £20 and £100. The average cost as of 2021 seems to be around £50 per therapy hour. You may discuss with your therapist if you think this work will be short-term (from six to twelve sessions) or longer term, but you will probably be in therapy for at least six sessions, so it is worth budgeting for between £120 and £600 for the first six sessions, depending on how much your chosen therapist charges.

If you find a therapist that you'd love to work with but you find their cost prohibitive, or if you can't afford the rates of anybody local to you, it is always worth explaining a little about your circumstances and asking if there are concessionary rates. Many therapists hold spaces back to offer them to those who would otherwise not be able to afford therapy. Many therapists will also let you space out your sessions to one hour every two weeks, which is often more affordable without necessarily breaking the flow of sessions. It is also worth considering teletherapy, which is therapy conducted over the phone or online using software, such as Zoom – this is often slightly cheaper for you, as there are usually no office rent costs for the therapist to pay.

Another way to find a therapist is to get in touch with your local branch of a mental health organization. There are many available, such as Mind, Relate, Rethink Mental Illness, and Turning Point, and they usually offer low-cost or free therapy. This tends to be short-term therapy and there's often a waiting list, but you may have more choice of the kind of therapy you receive and the wait times may be less severe than on the NHS.

How to Find a Great Therapist for You

Another of the benefits of seeking private therapy is that you can choose which practitioner you see. This means you can find someone who specializes in the issues you'd like help with. Being able to choose your therapist also means you can choose someone with a therapeutic modality and personality that you feel you can work best with.

One way to find a therapist is to use an online directory. With many online directories, you can filter practitioners by their sexuality and gender. The Pink Therapy directory in particular can filter practitioners by country, county/state, sexual identity, gender identity, clients they work with, and the modality of their approach. This can be really useful if you're looking for a trans therapist, which might make you feel more comfortable and less like you're having to constantly explain integral parts of your identity instead of talking through your issues.

Before you go into what could be a long-term therapeutic relationship, it's okay to contact several therapists that you think you can work with and see which of them feels like the best fit for you. Your potential therapists should be open to almost any questions or concerns that you have, so feel free to ask about how they work, whether they are accessible to you, and what they can offer you. It's important that you trust your therapist to treat you well and that you choose someone you feel you can comfortably share your issues with, so take all the time you need in this process.

Here are several great questions to ask any potential therapists to see if they are the right match for you. Some of these questions are inspired by Michael Bettinger's book *It's Your Hour* (2001), some have been asked to me as a therapist, and some I've picked up from different therapists and clients over time.

- Have you had any specific training in working with transgender and/or non-binary people? (Many therapy courses do not have specific training regarding LGBTQ+ and GSRD (gender, sexuality, and relationship diversity) clients, so it may be prudent to find a therapist who has sought extra training in how best to care for transgender people.)

- Have you worked with transgender and/or non-binary clients before? (This will often be listed on the therapist's website or directory entry, but it can be worth asking for a little more information.)

- What's your confidentiality policy? (A good therapist should be very willing to talk you through this.)

- How do you feel about taking medicine for mental health? (A good answer might be that they understand there are benefits and side effects, and would support you if you choose to take any medication without pushing you to start or stop.)

- How do you work to make your therapy practice anti-racist, anti-transphobic, and anti-oppression? (Having a good therapy practice means working to break down aspects of society that harm people. Working on an individual's issues without acknowledging how they have been affected by society is not good practice.)

- What would you do if you didn't understand part of a client's identity? (It's a common experience to feel like you have to spend a lot of time giving your therapist a Gender 101 lesson when you could be working through your issues. An effective therapist will be interested in how your identity uniquely affects your life but will not expect you to train them on the basics! If there's something they don't understand about your identity, they might instead put a 'pin' in the discussion and come back to it next session having done more research and training on the topic.)

- Do you believe that sexual orientation or gender can be changed through therapy? (Anyone who believes in conversion therapy is not for you!)

- Do you believe non-binary, transgender, and/or queer people can live full and satisfying lives? (Whatever your specific goals, they'll tie in to you living your best life. Any mental health professional who thinks LGBTQ+ people can't be fully happy won't help you get there.)

- What jobs or careers have you had before (or during) working as a therapist? (This can help you to get a feel for your therapist's interests, personality, and skills.)

- Have you had any complaints filed against you with any professional ethics organizations? (It can be helpful to know if your prospective therapist has broken any rules or harmed any clients in the past.)

If you choose to ask your therapists any questions, even if it's just whether or not they're able to take you on right now, it's important that your potential therapist is open and honest with their answers and clear about their boundaries.

The relationship between you and your therapist is going to be an important one. So much research has shown that a mutually respectful, caring, open, and honest relationship between the therapist and client is the most impactful and effective way to make therapeutic changes for the client (Lambert and Barley 2001; Sauer *et al.* 2010; Goldfried 2013; Stamoulos *et al.* 2016). If you don't feel like the vibe between you and your therapist is quite right, it's okay to try to find a therapist that you get on well with. This is not to say that you shouldn't expect challenges from your counsellor nor that you will always agree with what they have to say – more that, when challenges and ruptures in the relationship occur, it's important that you have a counsellor that you feel comfortable addressing this with.

It might also be worth asking yourself some questions after your initial meeting with your therapist, whether as a journal exercise or just by mulling them over for a while. Here are some questions that you might find useful to ask yourself.

- How comfortable did you feel when talking to the therapist? Did you feel your identities and perspectives were treated with respect?

- Did you feel that the therapist understood what you were saying and understood your point of view?

- Did you understand what the therapist was telling you? If there were any misunderstandings, did the therapist explain themselves warmly in a way you understood?

- Were you able to say what you wanted to say, and did you feel supported by the therapist to follow the goals you want to follow?

- Did the therapist seem interested in what you wanted to say and engaged while you were talking?

- Are you looking forward to speaking to the therapist again?

A Whistle-Stop Tour of Some Therapeutic Modalities

When looking for a therapist or counsellor, you might find

yourself feeling overwhelmed by the different kinds of therapy available to you. Different therapeutic modalities can offer different structures and types of help that may focus on different aspects of your life. Here are a few that you might see come up often.

Person-centred therapy. This is the modality that this book is written from and that is practised by yours truly! Person-centred therapy is designed to work with the ways the client sees themself, with minimal interpretation from the therapist, to help them to 'self-actualize'. While the therapist might be an expert in specific counselling tools, the client is treated as the expert on their own personality and needs, and the aim is to work together to overcome issues via a strong therapeutic relationship. The therapist's job is to work with the client to help them grow and achieve their full potential (whatever this might look like to the client) while providing empathy, authenticity, and unconditional respect for the client. Sessions tend to last for about an hour and take place over a number of weeks or months, or even years. You might also see this described as client-centred therapy.

Cognitive Behavioural Therapy (CBT). CBT focuses on how thoughts and emotions are linked, and how changing one can affect the other. You may spend time separately examining your thoughts, emotions, physical feelings, and behaviours around an issue to see where changes for the better can be made. The practitioner might involve you in 'experiments' between sessions, where you gently test your limits and experience the outcome or where you work on breaking down issues that feel overwhelming into smaller parts. This is most often the type of therapy that will be offered by the NHS. Sessions tend to last between 30 minutes to an hour and take place over a limited time.

Dialectical Behavioural Therapy (DBT). This is a variant of CBT that is designed to work particularly well for people experiencing post-traumatic stress and the long-term effects of trauma. The practitioner will often teach clients skills to process 'extreme' emotions and behaviours, for example distress tolerance (dealing with uncomfortable events and feelings), interpersonal effectiveness (communicating well in relationships), and emotional regulation (changing the intensity of emotions). DBT is often practised in a group setting, where you may be one of multiple clients. Session times may vary depending on the practitioner and tend to occur over a limited time.

Psychodynamic therapy. In psychodynamic theory, much of what causes us pain is the 'shadow' side of deep-rooted trauma that feels too painful to examine and so is pushed into the unconscious of our thoughts. The therapist works through interpretation and analysis of what lies behind the issues that the client brings to the sessions in order to solve them. There is often a focus on how past events affect the client's thoughts and feelings in the present. Psychodynamic therapists might work with their client through dream analysis, free association (talking spontaneously without the need to be coherent or logical), therapeutic transference (talking to the therapist as if they were a person in the client's past), and clinical interpretation. Sessions often last between an hour and two hours, and often happen over a long period of time.

Transactional Analysis (TA). TA is adjacent to psychodynamic and person-centred modalities. There is a focus on helping the client grow by analysing how they interact with others and with the different 'parts' of themselves, which are known as ego states (often represented as the inner parent, adult, and child). There is often a focus on the client's childhood relationships and the ways in which these have impacted the client's adult behaviours, communication styles, relationships, and overall personality. TA therapists often help clients to examine the patterns and scripts that they have learned in the past and that are not helpful in the present, and to redecide how they'd like their life to go. Sessions usually last for about an hour and tend to be medium- to long-term in duration.

Eye Movement Desensitization and Reprocessing (EMDR). This type of therapy is often used to help clients process unresolved trauma. It aims to help clients process difficult memories by revisiting past events as fully as possible while engaging in 'bilateral stimulation', aka moving a part of both sides of your body in an easy rhythm. This bilateral stimulation might involve tapping your hands on your knees one after the other or following a light from left to right with your eyes. The practitioner will work with you to fully explore memories, thoughts, and feelings regarding past trauma while ensuring you are currently in a safe place. Sessions tend to last for around an hour and are limited in number.

Emotional Freedom Technique (EFT or Tapping). This style of counselling works to unblock emotional pain and any associated physical discomfort, as well as reduce stress, by tapping on specific parts of the head and body while talking about an issue. An EFT practitioner may summarize the issue, ask how intense your feelings are about it, and ask you to say a specific phrase while tapping various 'pressure points'. This phrase may sound something like, 'Even though I'm experiencing this issue, I love and accept myself as I am.' The practitioner may then ask if the intensity of your feelings has changed after this process and repeat or move on from there. Session times and duration tend to vary, depending on the issue and the practitioner.

Integrative therapy. This style of therapy means the practitioner uses ideas, techniques, and elements from different therapeutic modalities. Most therapists will integrate different ideas and techniques in to their style of therapy, but an integrative therapist may specifically seek a blend of particular types of therapeutic modalities to create their own holistic method.

Coaching. This isn't quite the same as therapy, but it is a therapeutic relationship that involves a trained professional talking and listening to clients in order to process goals and overcome present issues. Practitioners usually focus on helping clients to change their present behaviours for the better and to grow towards their goals. There is often a focus on empowerment, goal-setting, and positive transformation using techniques and guidance. Coaching is often useful if you're feeling pretty good and you want to feel even better or if you wish to focus on achieving specific life goals.

Long-Term Therapy vs Short-Term Therapy

Short-term therapy tends to last for six to twelve sessions, and it tends to happen under a closed contract (where you and your therapist agree to see each other for a set number of sessions). You're more likely to have short-term therapy if you seek more directive styles of therapy, like EMDR or CBT. Long-term therapy, meanwhile, can last for as long as you find it beneficial, often with an open contract between you and your therapist (where there's no set limit or restriction on how long you and your therapist have agreed to work together, but you will be invited to check in about whether you'd like to continue at regular intervals). Longer-term therapy tends to be more accessible if you're prepared to seek out private services, and it's more likely to be offered by person-centred and psychodynamic therapists.

There are many benefits to both short- and long-term therapy, depending on the kind of help you're looking for. Having the kind of deadline that can come with short-term therapy can help you to focus on an individual problem, while the open-ended nature of long-term therapy can give you the time to fully explore multiple issues. Ultimately, how long you want to see a mental health professional for is up to you.

Group Therapy

Most of the therapeutic modalities mentioned above are offered to individual clients and sometimes couples, polycules, and families. If this doesn't appeal to you, you might also want to explore the idea of group therapy. Group therapy can be very helpful if you find processing your thoughts easier when talking to others. It can also help if your social skills are something you would like to improve therapeutically and if you would benefit from feeling less alone with what you're going through. You also have to be very ready to share your issues with a group of people, which can be nerve-wracking and challenging but ultimately rewarding.

In group therapy, you are likely to be in a group of five to fifteen people who are processing similar issues to you. This will be led by one or more trained therapists who act as group facilitators, who should make sure everybody in the group gets a chance to share and take up space. You will be invited and encouraged to share your thoughts and feelings with no judgement from the other clients in the group. There tend to be strong boundaries around what can and can't be shared outside of the group, often in the form of a group contract, so that you know what you've said in the group therapy context stays confidential.

Group therapy is more likely to be offered to you if you approach a charity or government-funded organization (such as Mind) or with certain types of treatment offered by the NHS (like DBT).

Helplines, Chatlines, and Hotlines

Helplines, where you talk to trained helpers on the phone, and chatlines, where you type to trained helpers in chat boxes online, can be helpful ways to process your emotions for a short amount of time. These services are usually run by trained volunteers who have specific training in areas of mental health related to the helpline. They can also offer information, resources, and signposting that can continue to help you. You can often stay anonymous when you access a helpline or chatline, so this can be a good tactic if you worry about being outed as transgender, and you can often access help quickly, which makes them handy in a crisis.

In the UK, the National Trans 24hr Helpline and Switchboard LGBT+ Helpline are both expressly trans-friendly support helplines equipped to help whether you are looking for advice, support, or signposting to other services, or you find yourself in a crisis.

If you are in the UK, you can also call 111 for help in a pinch. They may be able to signpost you to suitable services or, if they feel you need extra help in a crisis, they may send an ambulance or First Response Service to your whereabouts.

Forums, Support Groups, Coffee Mornings, and Other Peer Support

Peer-run community resources can be a real lifeline. You can be fairly certain that you will be speaking to other people with lived experience of the issue you'd like to explore. This can be excellent if you're worried about explaining the intricacies of who you are and what you've been through to get help – people who have experienced a life like yours will probably need less of an explanation, or you should at least be able to skip the 101.

Support groups can be run by charities, by community organizations, or by individuals who see a necessity for them. They can take many shapes, from a relaxed monthly coffee morning in a local cafe to a more formal ticketed event in a charity space.

Online, finding a forum can be an excellent source of community. If this seems kind of old school, support groups and community groups are popping up all the time (as of 2021) on apps like Discord, a free app geared towards online community chats. Facebook is also a good place to search for groups specific to your community needs – there are many trans-friendly groups for mental health and societal issues that you can join. You can also find community groups in some potentially unexpected places, such as Twitch, a livestreaming service that centres watching people play video games but also features people hosting support communities or just chatting to viewers.

If you're struggling to get out to find in-person peer support, a lot of support groups, coffee mornings, and peer-support are also available through communication software, such as Zoom and Google Hangouts.

Further Reading, Online Resources, and Other Sources of Information

Note: All of the resources shared here are all active and accurate as of 2021.

Recommended Further Reading

Here is a selection of books that have helped me to improve my own mental health and some that have been recommended to me by friends and therapy clients. You'll find a breadth of topics and voices here, with most of the writers being trans or otherwise LGBTQ+.

Anti-Diet: Reclaim Your Time, Money, Well-Being, and Happiness, by Christy Harrison – A well-researched and accessible book that's a great read if you're interested in improving your mental health and nourishing yourself, no matter what size you are.

Body Respect: What Conventional Health Books Get Wrong, Leave Out, and Just Plain Fail to Understand about Weight, by Lindo Bacon and Lucy Aphramor – Another excellent book about how you can focus on good health and body image at any size, this time by two non-binary authors.

Growing Older as a Trans and/or Non-Binary Person: A Support Guide, by Jennie Kermode – An important and much-needed guide to ageing as a trans person, written by a non-binary writer.

Health at Every Size: The Surprising Truth About Your Weight, by Lindo Bacon – Another classic by Lindo Bacon, helping you to eat and move in joyful and nourishing ways without dieting or restriction.

How to Understand Your Gender: A Practical Guide for Exploring Who You Are, by Alex Iantaffi and Meg-John Barker – A non-binary-led, reflective, and practical guide to figuring out what's going on with your gender. I've recommended this to clients in the past and it's been helpful for me, too!

Non-Binary Lives: An Anthology of Intersecting Identities, edited by Jos Twist, Ben Vincent, Meg-John Barker, and Kat Gupta – A collection of essays from all kinds of non-binary people and a great slice of non-binary lives.

Not Just a Tomboy: A Trans Masculine Memoir, by Caspar Baldwin – An inspiring and accessible memoir about a trans boy growing up to be a man in the 1990s and onwards. This is a great book to show loved ones who can't wrap their heads around what it means to be a trans man.

Person-Centred Counselling in Action, by Dave Mearns and Brian Thorne – This is a book written for therapy trainees and practitioners, but if you're looking for more of an insight into what person-centred therapy is all about, this is a must-read.

The Body Is Not an Apology: The Power of Radical Self-Love, by Sonya Renee Taylor – An exploration of how to offer yourself and your body compassion in the face of oppression and shame.

The Body Keeps the Score: Mind, Brain, and Body in the Transformation of Trauma, by Bessel van der Kolk – A classic examination of the effects of trauma and how to work with yourself (and others) to move forward.

The Carl Rogers Reader, by Howard Kirschenbaum and Valerie Henderson – The person-centred bible! This is a fascinating look at the life and work of the originator of person-centred theory and practice. It's well worth a look if you're curious about Rogers and how person-centred therapy came into being.

The Dialectical Behaviour Therapy Skills Workbook: Practical DBT Exercises for Learning Mindfulness, Interpersonal Effectiveness, Emotion Regulation, and Distress Tolerance, by Jeffrey Brantley, Jeffrey C. Wood, and Matthew McKay – A DBT workbook with lots of reflective questions and practical advice to help you navigate overwhelming emotions.

The Queer and Transgender Resilience Workbook: Skills for Navigating Sexual Orientation and Gender Expression, by Anneliese Singh – A workbook packed full of kind advice for how to be confident in a world that wants to take that from you. This one's been useful for me and my clients time and time again.

They/Them/Theirs: A Guide to Nonbinary and Genderqueer Identities, by Eris Young – A comprehensive look into life as a non-binary person, including our language, history, relationships, and more. This would also make a perfect gift for anyone who doesn't 'get it'.

Trans Britain: Our Journey From the Shadows, edited by Christine Burns – An interesting look at trans lives through British history, including activism, laws, visibility, and first-hand accounts of historical events.

Trans Like Me, by CN Lester – A thoughtful and knowledgeable book from a trans author about what it's really like to be trans, breaking down misconceptions about 'gender politics' along the way.

Trans Power: Own Your Gender, by Juno Roche – A revolutionary and intersectional take on what being trans really means and why being trans and/or non-binary makes us powerful.

Trauma and Recovery, by Judith Herman – A powerful and classic take on how trauma affects the body, the mind, and society, and what we can do about it.

Uncomfortable Labels: My Life as a Gay Autistic Trans Woman, by Laura Kate Dale – A memoir about the life of a gay autistic trans woman and how the intersections of our different identities affect us all.

Yes, You Are Trans Enough: My Transition from Self-Loathing to Self-Love, by Mia Violet – A memoir by a bi trans woman recounting her journey towards self-acceptance and a personal understanding of what it means to be 'trans enough' to be transgender.

Yoga for Everyone: 50 Poses for Every Type of Body, by Dianne Bondy – An incredibly inclusive guide to yoga, allowing you to build up a stretching and strength routine that actually works with your body and mind.

You and Your Gender Identity: A Guide to Discovery, by Dara Hoffman-Fox – A kind and helpful guide that encourages you to explore your gender and beyond through preparation, reflection, and exploration. This is another book that I've been happy to read and recommend to clients many times.

Online Resources

Here's a selection of websites, apps, and online games that I can recommend if you're looking for further help with your mental health.

#SelfCare – A free app that encourages calmness and self-kindness with short, gentle games, such as picking up virtual laundry and petting your virtual cat.

Aloe Bud – A free app designed to help you set manageable daily self-care goals, such as taking a deep breath, having something to drink, or thinking about something you're grateful for.

BlackOut UK – A social collective that supports Black, queer men in the UK. blkoutuk.com

Black Trans Alliance – An alliance offering peer support, advice, and advocacy to Black trans people in London and online. http://blacktransalliance.org

Blurt – A company aiming to increase awareness and understanding of depression by sharing free and paid-for resources. Blurt also runs a monthly subscription box of self-care surprises, which I can personally recommend if you have the money! http://blurtitout.org

Daylio – A free app designed to help you track your daily mood and self-care activities, with an option to write short journal entries.

Decolonizing Fitness, by Ilya Parker – Inclusive, affirming, weight-neutral fitness training resources by a Black non-binary trainer. http://decolonizingfitness.com

doddlevloggle, by dodie – A YouTube channel by Dodie Clark, AKA bisexual musician 'dodie', documenting her experiences of depersonalization, derealization, anxiety, and depression, as well as sharing videos about her life and music. www.youtube.com/user/doddlevloggle/featured

Emotional Baggage Check – Anonymously tell someone how you're feeling and what you're going through online, and receive a kind message back. You can also be the anonymous person who sends a kind message to a stranger. www.emotionalbaggagecheck.com

Forest – A free app designed to help you focus by rewarding you if you stay off your phone for a set amount of time. Forest commits to planting real trees when you meet certain goals.

Future Me – A website where you can write a letter to your future self, and receive it either one year or five years in the future. http://futureme.org

Gottman Card Decks – A free app with simple games and questions to help you bond with your partner(s), friends, and family.

Insight Timer – A free app (with a paid premium option) offering a huge amount of varied meditations.

Stay Alive – A free app designed to offer help if you're in crisis and to help you to prepare for future crises.

Podcasts

Here's a selection of podcasts on various trans-related, mental-health-related, and trans-adjacent mental health topics that can help you to feel held, seen, gently informed, and entertained. There are several amazing trans podcasters on this list!

Body Kindness, by Rebecca Scritchfield.

Gender Reveal, by Tuck Woodstock.

How to Fail, by Elizabeth Day.

I Am. I Have, by Happiful.

Who Hurt You?, by Sofie Hagen.

Meditation Minis, by Chel Hamilton.

Mental Health Mukbang, by the Asian Mental Health Collective.

Psych and the City, by Sarah Kelleher.

Queers & Co. Podcast, by Gem Kennedy.

Speaking of Psychology, by the American Psychological Association.

Stuck Not Broken, by Justin Sunseri.

System Speak, by Emma Sunshaw.

The GenderGP Podcast, by GenderGP.

The Meditation Podcast, by Jesse Stern and Jeane Stern.

The Savvy Psychologist's Quick and Dirty Tips for Better Mental Health, by Jade Wu.

The SelfWork Podcast, by Margaret Robinson Rutherford.

Therapy for Black Girls, by Joy Harden Bradford.

They/Them/Theirs, by Rayne and Casey.

What the Trans!?, by Michelle Snow and Ashleigh Talbot.

Communities

There are a real mixture of communities here, from online to IRL, short-term to long-term, local to worldwide, and connecting two people or hundreds. You can get involved in community in whatever way suits you.

Bent Bars – A grassroots letter-writing project aiming to help incarcerated LGBTQ+ people in Great Britain feel connected, by connecting them with pen pals outside of prison. www.bentbarsproject.org

Cara-Friend – An LGBTQ+ organization in Northern Ireland that runs youth groups. www.cara-friend.org.uk

First Person Plural – An online association for those experiencing dissociative identity disorders, offering resources and support. www.firstpersonplural.org.uk

Free2B – A community organization in London that offers group and one-to-one social spaces for trans young people and their parents. www.free2b-alliance.org.uk

Glitter Cymru – A monthly meet-up group in South Wales for LGBTQ+ BAME (Black, Asian and minority ethnic) people. @GlitterCymru on Twitter.

Imaan Forum – An online forum community for LGBTQ+ Muslim individuals. www.forum.imaan.org.uk

Kamp Kiki – UK-based retreats for trans and/or non-binary adults from the African and Caribbean Diaspora. You can get involved with creative writing, meditation, dancing, therapy, and more. www.humblebeecreativeltd.com

MindOut – A community space in Brighton offering peer support groups, peer mentoring, self-advocacy workshops, and online support. www.mindout.org.uk

Opening Doors London – A charity offering a befriending service to LGBTQ+ people over the age of 50 in London. They also offer a befriending service over the phone for those outside of London. www.openingdoorslondon.org.uk

Sparkle Weekend – A yearly event for the trans community held in the summer in Manchester, England. Run by The National Transgender Charity. www.sparkle.org.uk

Stef Sanjati's stream on Twitch – A Twitch channel where you can watch Stef Sanjati – a trans, bisexual change-maker – play video games. There is a strong trans presence in the group, with a commitment to cosiness and emotional safety. https://m.twitch.tv/thestefsanjati/profile

The Asian Mental Health Collective – A worldwide collective that aspires to make mental health easily accessible to Asian communities. They offer online support and resources, including the Mental Health Mukbang podcast. www.asianmhc.org

Charities, Helplines, and Other Free Advice

Note: All of the resources shared here are all active and accurate as of 2021.

Therapy Funds

Here's a small selection of funds set up to help people access therapy for free or at a low cost to the client. Most of these funds are specially designed for Black trans and/or non-binary people. I firmly believe that therapy is for everyone, including and especially the most marginalized of us, and the mental health of Black transfeminine people in particular should be protected. I hope these funds can make therapy more accessible to those who need it most.

Black LGBTQIA+ Therapy Fund, by Rose Frimpong. @BlackLGBTFund on Twitter.

Black Trans Free Therapy Fund, by Axelle Nasah. @BlackTransUK on Twitter.

Radical Therapist Network QTBPOC Therapy Fund, by Radical Therapist Network. www.radicaltherapistnetwork.com/qtibipoc-therapy-fund

The Empowerment Group (offering two pathways for funded applications: 'BAME Therapy' and 'Therapy for All'). www.theempowermentgroup.co.uk

Charities and Free Services

This list includes free help for trans people seeking different kinds of assistance with well-being. There's support here from gentle self-care advice to intense residential treatment, all of which have been vetted as trans-friendly.

56T – A trans-led holistic sexual health and well-being service for trans and/or non-binary people and their partners, located at Dean Street in London. Services include sexual health screening, liver function tests, PrEP (pre-exposure prophylaxis), hepatitis testing, cervical smears, advice, and counselling. Open Wednesdays 4:30–7pm. www.dean.st/trans-non-binary

akt (Albert Kennedy Trust) – A UK-based trust that aims to support LGBTQ+ young people aged 16–25, particularly those who are homeless or in difficult housing situations. www.akt.org.uk

Black Minds Matter UK – A UK-based charity offering free 12-week courses of therapy to Black individuals over the age of 16. www.blackmindsmatteruk.com

Books Beyond Bars – A collective of volunteers who send free books, zines, and activities to incarcerated LGBTQ+ people in the UK. www.beyond-bars.org

Drayton Park Women's Crisis Service – A week-long residential support service for adult women experiencing a mental health crisis who live in Camden or Islington, London. They are explicitly accepting of trans and/or non-binary women. There is a mix of formal and informal support and crisis interventions offered. You can self-refer by calling 020 7607 2777.

East London Out Project – A project offering social support and counselling for LGBTQ+ people in East London. www.elop.org

Gendered Intelligence – A UK-based support organization working with young trans people. www.genderedintelligence.co.uk

GenderJam NI – A charity based in Belfast that supports trans people in Northern Ireland. www.transgenderni.org.uk

GIRES (Gender Identity Research and Education) – A UK-based charity that provides information and research for trans people, their families, and the medical professionals who work with them. www.gires.org.uk

Grassroots – A suicide prevention charity working in Brighton and across the UK. They offer training, community, and support. www.prevent-suicide.org.uk

LGBT Foundation – A Manchester-based charity offering support to LGBTQ+ people. www.lgbt.foundation

LGBT Youth Scotland – A charity working with LGBTQ+ youth in Scotland, who are between the ages of 13 and 25. www.lgbtyouth.org.uk

London Friend – A charity supporting the mental and emotional health of LGBTQ+ people in and around London. www.london-friend.org.uk

Maytree – A charity offering residential suicide respite centre for adults in London, allowing safe, non-medical support for five days. You can self-refer by emailing maytree@maytree.org.uk or calling 020 7263 7070.

Mermaids – A UK-based, ally-run charity that aims to support young trans children up to the age of 19. www.mermaidsuk.org.uk

MIND – A charity offering free therapy, community groups, helplines, advice, and more across the UK. www.mind.org.uk

QueerCare – A transfeminist, charitable, community care organization providing training, support, and advocacy for trans and queer people in the UK. https://queercare.network

Rethink Mental Illness – A UK-based charity providing advice and support to people living with mental illness and those that care for them. www.rethink.org

Spectra – A London-based charity for LGBTQ+ people that aims to increase access to support and well-being. www.spectra-london.org.uk

Stonewall – A UK-based charity offering support, training, advocacy, and resources for trans people, allies, and organizations. www.stonewall.org.uk

TASSN (Trans Asylum Seeker Support Network) – A direct action and mutual aid collective focused on supporting trans asylum seekers, specifically helping them to get out of US Immigration and Customs Enforcement (ICE) detention and helping them build thriving lives. www.givebutter.com/tassn

The Rainbow Project – A charity in Northern Ireland working to improve the physical, mental, and emotional well-being of LGBTQ+ people. www.rainbow-project.org

Turning Point – A UK-based charity providing mental health support to individuals with learning disabilities and complex care needs, including drug and alcohol support. www.turning-point.co.uk

Helplines

Here is a selection of helplines, textlines, and online chat services that support people with different mental health needs. Some are useful if you just need to let someone know how you're feeling, and some are equipped to offer you support if you're in crisis. Either way, you'll find someone to reach out to here.

Cara-Friend – An LGBTQ+ organization, email service, and helpline in Northern Ireland. Call 0808 8000 390 or email switchboard@ cara-friend.org.uk. Open Monday–Friday 1–4pm, plus Wednesdays 6–9pm.

FRANK – An advisory help service designed to give honest information and advice about drugs, substance misuse, and how to get help. Call 0300 123 6600, text 82111, or email through the website at www.talktofrank.com. Open 24/7.

Galop's LGBT+ Hate Crime Helpline – A helpline and email service that supports people who have survived a hate crime. Call 020 7704 2040, or email hatecrime@galop.org.uk. Open Monday–Friday, 10am–4pm.

Galop's National Lesbian, Gay, Bisexual and Trans+ Domestic Abuse Helpline – A helpline and email service for LGBTQ+ people who have survived, or are surviving, domestic abuse. Call 0800 999 5428, or email help@galop.org.uk. Open Monday, Tuesday and Friday 10am–5pm, and Wednesday–Thursday 10am–8pm.

LGBT Helpline Scotland – A helpline for LGBTQ+ people living in Scotland. Call 0300 123 2523. Open Tuesdays 12–9pm, Wednesdays 12–9pm, Thursdays 1–6pm, and Sundays 1–6pm.

LGBT Youth Scotland – A text helpline for LGBT youth in Scotland. Text 07984 356 512. Open weekdays.

Mermaids – A UK-based helpline, run by allies, for young trans people in need of support. Call 0808 8010 400.

MindLine Trans+ – A UK-based helpline for trans and/or non-binary people in need of support. Call 03003305468. Open Monday – Friday 8pm – midnight.

National Trans 24hr Helpline – A helpline to support all trans, non-binary, questioning, and intersex people in the UK, 24 hours a day and every day of the year. Call 07527 524 034.

Papyrus – A UK helpline, textline, and email service that specifically helps suicidal young people. Call 0800 068 4141, text 07786 209 697, or email pat@papyrus-uk.org. Open Monday–Friday 10am–10pm, plus weekends and bank holidays 2–5pm.

SANEline – A helpline and email service offering advice and support to anyone aged 16 and over who is experiencing mental health difficulties in the UK. Call 0300 304 7000, or email support@sane.org.uk. Open Monday–Friday 12–11pm and weekends 12–6pm.

Shelter – A helpline for urgent housing advice. Call 0808 800 4444. Open Monday–Friday 8am–8pm and weekends 9am–5pm.

SignHealth – A textline for Deaf and/or deaf people in crisis. Text DEAF to 85258. Open 24/7.

SurvivorsUK – UK-based online and text support for all kinds of men who are survivors of sexual abuse. Text 020 3322 1860 or visit www.survivorsuk.org. Open every day, 12–8pm.

Switchboard LGBT+ Helpline – A UK helpline for LGBT+ people that's run by LGBT+ people. Call 0300 330 0630, email chris@switchboard. lgbt, or text 'Switchboard' to 85258. Open 10am–10pm every day.

Trans Lifeline – A US peer support phone service run by and for trans people. Call (877) 565-8860 or visit translifeline.org.

Counselling Associations

These associations regulate and inform counsellors and psycho-therapists in the UK. If you're looking to make sure a prospective therapist is trained and practising ethically, they'll be a member of some kind of register – these are the most common. On the websites for these associations you'll find their ethical guidelines and some information about their regulations.

British Association for Counselling and Psychotherapy (BACP) – A governing body for counsellors and psychotherapists in Britain. They also have a directory for BACP registered counsellors who have demonstrated that they meet BACP standards, meaning they have passed a competency and ethics exam run by BACP. www.bacp.co.uk

The National Counselling Society (NCS) – A regulating body for counsellors in the UK. They have a directory for NCS-accredited counsellors. www.nationalcounsellingsociety.org

United Kingdom Council for Psychotherapy (UKCP) – A regulating body for psychotherapists in Britain. They also have a directory for UKCP members. www.psychotherapy.org.uk

Therapy Directories

This list of therapy directories can help you to find the right therapist for you. You can search these directories for therapists who meet your specific requirements, for example filtering by gender, ethnicity, price range, and modality.

BAATN *(The Black, African and Asian Therapy Network)* – A UK-based directory of therapists of Black, African, South Asian, and Caribbean heritage. www.baatn.org.uk

Counselling Directory – A popular UK-based directory for mental health professionals. www.counselling-directory.org.uk

MCAPN (Muslim Counsellor and Psychotherapist Network) – A worldwide directory for Muslim counsellors, psychotherapists, psychiatrists, and counselling psychologists. www.mcapn.co.uk

Pink Therapy –A worldwide directory for mental health workers who work with LGBTQ+ clients. They also offer training specifically for GSRD clients and therapists. www.pinktherapy.com

Psychology Today – A worldwide directory that can help you find a mental health professional or support group. You can search for practitioners by their sexuality and gender. www.psychologytoday.com

Bye For Now

If You Read This Book Because
Things Are Really Hard

If things are really hard for you right now, I also know how difficult it can be to believe that you can do this. When you hear stories about how other people have changed their lives for the better, it's totally normal to believe that you're different, that you can't do what they've done, that it's too hard for you, or that your circumstances are too different. I promise you that you can do this. You can find support, you can engage in whatever self-care suits you, and you can change your circumstances for the better. You might need to look beyond what you thought was possible to do this, and to engage in aspects of caring for yourself that you said you'd never try, but this kind of commitment to change what you formerly thought of as impossible can be what gives you the most room to grow and heal. Every day, I see people in your position move forwards towards the lives they truly want to lead. I've seen people, including myself, move through the worst of times and onwards to peace, happiness, and stability.

You have the tools and the words in this book to help

you whenever you need them and so much more besides. You have whatever resilience has kept you here so far. You have a community who wants to know what you have to say. You are so worthy of love and care, and I'm glad you're here to read thi today.

If You Read This Book Because You Wanted to Keep Improving Your Mental Health

If things aren't so hard for you right now, and you picked up this book to keep things that way, keep going! You're doing amazing things and now you (hopefully) have some new ideas from this book that can make things even better. There is always more to discover about who you are and what you can do – so keep looking after yourself and keep exploring yourself (and remember that this means taking a break from improving yourself, too – it's okay to just *be*). You can give yourself any kind of self-care that you need and make any kind of changes that you need, because you're absolutely worth it.

Some Final Thoughts

Through this book we've explored a lot together, including good mental health advice, practical therapeutic tips, and information that shows you're not alone. Through everything, my aim has been to hold your experience and gently inspire you to grow in any direction you feel will be good for you. I hope that I've managed to meet you where you are and give you a bit of a leg-up to where you want to be.

If there's anything I really want you to take away from this book, it's that you can make a change. It might feel impossible right now, or you might not know the right direction to move in, or you might know exactly what change you need to make but it seems so scary. Maybe there are people and circumstances that are stopping you from changing in the ways you need. The options in front of you might seem hopeless, unattainable, lonely, boring, or painful. It's so hard – I know; I've been there. I also know that it's possible to move through those difficult circumstances and emotions to get to where you need to be. Whether you're trying to pull yourself from the depth of depression or working to shrug off that last bit of anxiety, moving towards good mental health can also be liberating, exciting, fascinating, peaceful, and joyful – and you deserve that. You deserve all of the good things in the world, whether you had to fight for them or they came into your life completely spontaneously. You deserve good mental health, and you deserve to be here.

Hang in there, reader. Keep fighting the good fight. Remember that your rights are human rights and good mental health is for everyone. Remember that help is available, and that your trans siblings are with you. This book is also here with you right now, which means I'm with you, too, for as long as you need.

Take care! I believe in you!

References

Acharya, T. and Agius, M. (2017) 'The importance of hope against other factors in the recovery of mental illness.' *Psychiatria Danubina*, 29, 3, 619–622.

Al-Kadhi, A. (2018) 'Queer and transgender people are still taught to experience shame – here's what you can do to counter this.' *The Independent*. Accessed on 09/07/2021 at www.independent.co.uk/voices/transgender-queer-people-shame-how-counter-feelings-discrimination-coming-out-lgbtq-a8198621.html.

American Psychiatric Association (2013) *Diagnostic and Statistical Manual of Mental Disorders*, (5th edition). Arlington, VA: American Psychiatric Association.

Bachmann, C. L., Gooch, B., and Long, A. (2018) 'LGBT in Britain: Trans report.' London: Stonewall. Accessed on 09/07/2021 at www.stonewall. org.uk/system/files/lgbt_in_britain_-_trans_report_final.pdf.

Bacon, L. (2008) *Health at Every Size: The surprising truth about your weight.* Dallas, TX: BenBella Books.

Bacon, L. and Aphramor, L. (2011) 'Weight science: Evaluating the evidence for a paradigm shift.' *Nutrition Journal*, 10, 9, 1–13.

Bauer, G., Scheim, A., Pyne, J., Travers, R., and Hammond, R. (2015) 'Intervenable factors associated with suicide risk in transgender persons:

A respondent driven sampling study in Ontario, Canada.' *BMC Public Health*, 15, 525, 1–15.

Baumeister, R. F. and Leary, M. R. (1995) 'The need to belong: Desire for interpersonal attachments as a fundamental human motivation.' *Psychological Bulletin*, 117, 3, 497–529.

BBC (2013) 'The Great British class calculator.' Accessed on 09/07/2021 at www.bbc.co.uk/news/special/2013/newsspec_5093/index.stm.

Beck, A. T., Kovacs, M., and Weissman, A. (1979) 'Assessment of suicidal intention: The Scale for Suicide Ideation.' *Journal of Consulting and Clinical Psychology*, 47, 2, 343–352.

Becker, I., Auer, M., Barkmann, C., Fuss, J., *et al.* (2018) 'A cross-sectional multicenter study of multidimensional body image in adolescents and adults with gender dysphoria before and after transition-related medical interventions.' *Archives of Sexual Behaviour*, 47, 2335–2347.

Bettinger, M. (2001) *It's Your Hour: A Guide to Queer-affirmative Psychotherapy*. New York City: Alyson Publications Inc.

Bishop, G. J. (2017) *Unfuck Yourself: Get Out of Your Head and Into Your Life*. London: Yellow Kite.

Blackstock, C. (2011) 'The Emergence of the Breath of Life Theory.' *Journal of Social Work Values and Ethics*, 8, 1.

Boyes, A. (2018) *The Healthy Mind Toolkit: Simple Strategies to Get Out of Your Own Way and Enjoy Your Life*. New York City: Tarcherperigee.

Brantley, J., Wood, J. C., and McKay, M. (2007) *The Dialectical Behaviour Therapy Skills Workbook: Practical DBT exercises for learning mindfulness, interpersonal effectiveness, emotion regulation, and distress tolerance*. Oakland, CA: New Harbinger Publications.

Broadhead, W. E., Kaplan, B. H., James, S. A., and Wagner, E. H. (1983) 'The epidemiological evidence for a relationship between social support and health.' *American Journal of Epidemiology*, 117, 5, 521–537.

Brown, B. (2013) 'Shame Is Lethal.' *Super Soul Sunday*, Oprah Winfrey Network, season 4, episode 415. Accessed on 09/07/2021 at www.youtube.com/watch?v=GEBjNv5M784.

Buczynski, R. and Porges, S. W. (2012) 'Polyvagal theory: Why this changes everything.' *NICABM Trauma Therapy Series*. Accessed 24/04/2021 at www.flexiblemindtherapy.com/uploads/6/5/5/2/65520823/nicabm-porges-2012.pdf.

Butler, C., Joiner, R., Bradley, R., Bowles, M., *et al*. (2019) 'Self-harm prevalence and ideation in a community sample of cis, trans and other youth.' *International Journal of Transgenderism*, 20, 4, 447–458.

Cacioppo, J. T. and Cacioppo, S. (2014) 'Social relationships and health: The toxic effects of perceived social isolation.' *Social and Personality Psychology Compass*, 8, 2, 58–72.

Campos, P., Saguy, A., Ernsberger, P., Oliver, E., and Gaesser, G. (2006) 'The epidemiology of overweight and obesity: Public health crisis or moral panic?' *International Journal of Epidemiology*, 35, 1, 55–60.

Canaipa, R., Treister, R., Lang, M., Moreira, J. M., and Castro-Caldas, A. (2016) 'Feeling hurt: Pain sensitivity is correlated with and modulated by social distress.' *The Clinical Journal of Pain*, 32, 1, 14–19.

Cannon, W. (1932) *Wisdom of the Body*. New York City: W. W. Norton & Company.

Clance, P. R. and Imes, S. A. (1978) 'The impostor phenomenon in high achieving women: Dynamics and therapeutic intervention.' *Psychotherapy: Theory, Research and Practice*, 15, 3, 241–247.

Colizzi, M., Costa, R., and Todarello, O. (2015) 'Dissociative symptoms in individuals with gender dysphoria: is the elevated prevalence real?' *Psychiatry Research*, 226, 1, 173–180.

Compton, J. (2019) '"Frightening" online transphobia has real-life consequences, advocates say.' *NBC News*. Accessed on 09/07/2021 at www.nbcnews.com/feature/nbc-out/frightening-online-transphobia-has-real-life-consequences-advocates-say-n1089456.

Connolly, M. D., Zervos, M. J., Barone, C. J., Johnson, C. C., and Joseph, C. L. M. (2016) 'The mental health of transgender youth: Advances in understanding.' *Journal of Adolescent Health*, 59, 5, 489–495.

Cooper, M., and Dryden, W. (2015) *The Handbook of Pluralistic Counselling and Psychotherapy*. New York City: SAGE Publications Ltd.

Cooper, M., Mearns, D., Stiles, W. B., Warner, M., and Elliot, R. (2004) 'Developing self-pluralistic perspectives within the person-centered and experiential approaches: A round table dialogue.' *Person-Centered and Experiential Psychotherapies*, 3, 3, 176–191.

Costa, R. and Colizzi, M. (2016) 'The effect of cross-sex hormonal treatment on gender dysphoria individuals' mental health: A systematic review.' *Neuropsychiatric Disease and Treatment*, 12, 1953–1966.

Cross, T. (2007) 'Through Indigenous Eyes: Rethinking Theory and Practice.' *SNAICC Conference*. Accessed on 25/10/2021 at https://www.snaicc.org.au/through-indigenous-eyes-rethinking-theory-and-practice-keynote-address-2007-cross-t-snaicc-conf-2007-2.

Daley, A. (2021) 'The damaging impact of Western beauty standards.' *The Boar*. Accessed on 24/04/2021 at https://theboar.org/2021/01/damaging-impact-western-beauty.

Dana, D. (2018) *The Polyvagal Theory in Therapy: Engaging the rhythm of regulation*. New York City: W. W. Norton & Company.

Dana, D. (2020) *Polyvagal Exercises for Safety and Connection: 50 Client-Centred Practices*. New York City: W. W. Norton & Company.

Davies, J., Pitman, A., Bamber, V., Billings, J., and Rowe, S. (2020) 'Young peoples' perspectives on the role of harm reduction techniques in the management of their self-harm: A qualitative study.' *Archives of Suicide Research*. DOI: 10.1080/13811118.2020.1823916.

Dhejne, C., Van Vlerken, R., Heylens, G., and Arcelus, J. (2016) 'Mental health and gender dysphoria: A review of the literature.' *International Review of Psychiatry*, 28, 1, 44–57.

Dohrenwend, B. P. (1966) 'Social status and psychological disorder: An issue of substance and an issue of method.' *American Sociological Review*, 31, 14–34.

Dohrenwend, B. P. (2000) 'The role of adversity and stress in psychopathology:

Some evidence and its implications for theory and research.' *Journal of Health and Social Behaviour*, 41, 1–19.

Ellis, S., Bailey, J., and McNeil, J. (2015) 'Trans people's experiences of mental health and gender identity services: A UK study.' *Journal of Gay and Lesbian Mental Health*, 19, 1, 4–20.

Farhi, D. (1996) *The Breathing Book: Good Health and Vitality Through Essential Breath Work*. New York City: Holt (Henry) & Co.

Feltham, C. and Dryden, W. (1993) *Dictionary of Counselling*. Hoboken, NJ: John Wiley & Sons.

Fetzner, M. G. and Asmundson, G. J. (2015) 'Aerobic exercise reduces symptoms of posttraumatic stress disorder: A randomized controlled trial.' *Cognitive Behaviour Therapy*, 44, 4, 301–313.

Fink, G. (2016) 'In retrospect: Eighty years of stress.' *Nature*, 539, 7628, 175–176.

Firth, J. and Brewin, C. (1982) 'Attributions and recovery from depression: A preliminary study using cross-lagged correlation analysis.' *The British Journal of Clinical Psychology*, 21, 3, 229–230.

FRA (2012) *LGBI Survey 2012*. Accessed on 24/04/2012 at https://fra.europa.eu/en/publication/2013/eu-lgbt-survey-european-union-lesbian-gay-bisexual-and-transgender-survey results.

FRA (2020) *A Long Way To Go For LGBTI Equality*. Accessed on 09/07/2021 at https://fra.europa.eu/en/publication/2020/eu-lgbti-survey-results.

Froreich, F. V., Vartanian, L. R., Grisham, J. R., and Touyz, S. W. (2016) 'Dimensions of control and their relation to disordered eating behaviours and obsessive-compulsive symptoms.' *Journal of Eating Disorders*. 4, 1.

Gleming, M. Z., MacGowan, B. R., Robinson, L., Spitz, J., and Salt, P. (1982) 'The body image of the postoperative female-to-male transsexual.' *Journal of Consulting and Clinical Psychology*, 50, 3, 461–462.

Glynn, T.R. and van den Berg, J. J. (2017) 'A systematic review of interventions to reduce problematic substance use among transgender individuals: A call to action.' *Transgender Health*, 2, 1, 45–59.

Goldfried, M. R. (2013) 'What should we expect from psychotherapy?' *Clinical Psychology Review, 33*, 862–869.

Gómez-Gil, E., Zubiaurre-Elorza, L., Esteva, I., Guillamon, A., *et al.* (2012) 'Hormone-treated transsexuals report less social distress, anxiety and depression.' *Psychoneuroendocrinology, 37*, 5, 662–670.

Grant, J. M., Mottet, L. A., Tanis, J., Harrison, J. L., Herman, J. L., and Keisling, M. (2011) *Injustice at Every Turn: A Report of the National Transgender Discrimination Survey.* Accessed on 09/07/2021 at www.transequality. org/sites/default/files/docs/resources/NTDS_Report.pdf.

Green and Black Cross (2017) *Being Trans and Protesting.* Accessed on 09/07/2021 at https://greenandblackcross.org/wp-content/uploads/2017/06/Being-Trans-and-Protesting-Protest-Key-Information.pdf.

Harrison, C. (2019) *Anti-Diet: Reclaim Your Time, Money, Well-Being, and Happiness.* London: Yellow Kite.

Hendricks, M. L. and Testa, R. J. (2012) 'A conceptual framework for clinical work with transgender and gender nonconforming clients: An adaptation of the Minority Stress Model.' *Professional Psychology: Research and Practice, 43*, 5, 460–467.

Herman, J. (1992) *Trauma and Recovery: The Aftermath of Violence – From Domestic Abuse to Political Terror.* New York City: Basic Books.

Hillebrandt, H., Sebastian, C., and Blakemore, S. J. (2011) 'Experimentally induced social inclusion influences behavior on trust games.' *Cognitive Neuroscience, 2*, 1, 27–33.

Hirsch, C. R. and Holmes, E. A. (2007) 'Mental imagery in anxiety disorders.' *Psychiatry, 6*, 4, 161–165.

Hobbes, M. and MacKay, F. (2018) 'Everything You Know About Obesity Is Wrong.' *Huffington Post.* Accessed on 09/07/2021 at https://highline. huffingtonpost.com/articles/en/everything-you-know-about-obesity-is-wrong.

Hoffman-Fox, D. (2017) *You and Your Gender Identity: A Guide to Discovery.* New York: Skyhorse Publishing.

Hope, S. (2019) *Person-Centred Counselling for Trans and Gender Diverse People: A Practical Guide.* London: Jessica Kingsley Publishers.

Hopper, J. W., Frewen, P. A., van der Kolk, B. A., and Lanius, R. A. (2007) 'Neural correlates of reexperiencing, avoidance, and dissociation in PTSD: Symptom dimensions and emotion dysregulation in responses to script-driven trauma imagery.' *Journal of Traumatic Stress, 20*, 5, 713–725.

Hughto, J. M. W., Quinn, E. K., Dunbar, M. S., Rose, A. J., Shireman, T. I., and Jasuja, G. K. (2021) 'Prevalence and co-occurrence of alcohol, nicotine, and other substance use disorder diagnoses among US transgender and cisgender adults.' *Jama Network Open, 4*, 2.

Hunt, J. (2012) *Why the Gay and Transgender Population Experiences Higher Rates of Substance Use.* Center for American Progress. Accessed on 09/07/2021 at www.americanprogress.org/issues/lgbtq-rights/reports/2012/03/09/11228/why-the-gay-and-transgender-population-experiences-higher-rates-of-substance-use.

Hunte, B. (2019) 'Transgender people treated "inhumanely" online.' BBC News. Accessed on 09/07/2021 at www.bbc.co.uk/news/technology-50166900.

Jackson Levin, N., Kattari, S. K., Piellusch, E. K., and Watson, E. (2020) '"We just take care of each other". Navigating "chosen family" in the context of health, illness, and the mutual provision of care amongst queer and transgender young adults.' *International Journal of Environmental Research and Public Health, 8*, 17, 19, 7346.

Johnson, A. (2015) 'How understanding neuroscience helps me get unstuck.' *Schizophrenia Bulletin, 41*, 3, 544–545.

Johnson, B., Leibowitz, S., Chavez, A., and Herbert, S. E. (2019) 'Risk versus resiliency: Addressing depression in lesbian, gay, bisexual, and transgender youth.' *Child and Adolescent Psychiatric Clinics of North America, 28*, 3, 509–521.

Jones, Z. (2017) 'Depersonalization in gender dysphoria: Widespread and widely unrecognized.' *Gender Analysis with Zinnia Jones.* Accessed on 09/07/2021 at https://genderanalysis.net/2017/06/depersonalization-in-gender-dysphoria-widespread-and-widely-unrecognized.

Jones, Z. (2018) '5 things to know about transgender depersonalization.' *Gender Analysis with Zinnia Jones.* Accessed on 09/07/2021 at https://zinniajones.medium.com/5-things-to-know-about-transgender-depersonalization-8d0e27d29947.

Joorman, J., Siemer, M., and Gotlib, I. H. (2007) 'Mood regulation in depression: Differential effects of distraction and recall of happy memories on sad mood.' *Journal of Abnormal Psychology, 116,* 3, 484–490.

Keating, L. and Muller, R. T. (2019) 'LGBTQ+ based discrimination is associated with PTSD symptoms, dissociation, emotion dysregulation, and attachment insecurity among LGBTQ+ adults who have experienced Trauma.' *Journal of Trauma and Dissociation, 21,* 1, 124–141.

Kirschenbaum, H. and Henderson, V. L. (1990) *The Carl Rogers Reader.* Edinburgh: Robinson.

Klonsky, E. D., May, A. M., and Saffer, B. Y. (2016) 'Suicide, suicide attempts, and suicidal ideation.' *Annual Review of Clinical Psychology, 12,* 1, 307–330.

Knutson, D., Koch, J. M., Arthur, T., Mitchell, T. A., and Martyr, M. A. (2017) '"Trans broken arm": Health care stories from transgender people in rural areas.' *Journal of Research on Women and Gender, 7,* 30–46.

Krupnik, V. (2021) 'Tackling hyperarousal: An integrative multimodal approach.' *Cognitive Neuropsychiatry, 26,* 3, 199–212.

Lambert, M. J. and Barley, D. E. (2001) 'Research summary on the therapeutic relationship and psychotherapy outcome.' *Psychotherapy: Theory, Research, Practice, Training, 38,* 4, 357–361.

Levy, B. J. and Anderson, M. C. (2008) 'Individual differences in the suppression of unwanted memories: The executive deficit hypothesis.' *Acta Psychologica, 127,* 3, 623–625.

Li, Z., Wang, Y., Mao, X., and Yin, X. (2018) 'Relationship between hope and depression in college students: A cross-lagged regression analysis.' *Personality and Mental Health, 12,* 2, 170–176.

Liberty. (2021) *Practical Tips for Attending a Protest.* Accessed on 09/07/2021 at www.libertyhumanrights.org.uk.

Linehan, M. M. (2015) *DBT Skills Training Manual* (2nd edition). New York City: Guilford Press.

Link, B. G. and Phelan, J. C. (2001) 'Conceptualising stigma.' *Annual Review of Sociology, 27*, 363–385.

Lough Dennell, B. L., Anderson, G., and McDonnell, D. (2018) *Life In Scotland For LGBT Young People.* Accessed on 09/07/2021 at www.lgbtyouth.org.uk/media/1354/life-in-scotland-for-lgbt-young-people.pdf.

Maiden, R. J. (1987) 'Learned helplessness and depression: A test of the reformulated model.' *Journal of Gerontology, 42*, 1, 60–4.

Marshall, E., Claes, L., Bouman, W. P., Witcomb, G. L., and Arcelus, J. (2016) 'Non-suicidal self-injury and suicidality in trans people: A systematic review of the literature.' *International Review of Psychiatry, 28*, 158–169.

Maslow, A. (1943) 'A theory of human motivation.' *Psychological Review, 50*, 370–396.

McCullough, M., Tsang, J. A., and Emmons, R. A. (2004) 'Gratitude in intermediate affective terrain: Links of grateful moods to individual differences and daily emotional experience.' *Personality and Social Psychology, 86*, 2, 295–309.

McDermot, E., Hughes, E., and Rawlings, V. (2018) 'Norms and normalisation: Understanding lesbian, gay, bisexual, transgender and queer youth, suicidality and help-seeking.' *Culture, Health, and Sexuality, 20*, 2, 156–172.

McGuire, J. K., Doty, J. L., Catalpa, J. M., and Ola, C. (2016) 'Body image in transgender young people: Findings from a qualitative, community based study.' *Body Image, 18*, 96–107.

McNeil, J., Bailey, J., Ellis, S., Morton, J., and Regan, M. (2012) *Trans Mental Health Study 2012.* Accessed on 09/07/2021 at www.scottishtrans.org/wp-content/uploads/2013/03/trans_mh_study.pdf.

Mearns, D. and Thorne, B. (2000) *Person-Centred Counselling in Action.* London: SAGE Publications.

Meyer, I. H. (2003) 'Prejudice, social stress, and mental health in lesbian, gay, and bisexual populations: Conceptual issues and research evidence.' *Psychological Bulletin, 129*, 5, 674–697.

Meyer, I. H. (2015) 'Resilience in the study of minority stress and health of sexual and gender minorities.' *Psychology of Sexual Orientation and Gender Diversity, 2,* 3, 209–213.

Mueller, A., Quadros, C., Schwarz, K., Brandelli Costa, A., *et al.* (2016) 'Rumination as a marker of psychological improvement in transsexual women postoperative.' *Transgender Health, 1,* 1, 1, 274–278.

Mun, M., Gautam, M., Maan, R., and Krayem, B. (2020) 'An increased presence of male personalities in dissociative identity disorder after initiating testosterone therapy.' *Case Reports in Psychiatry.* DOI: 10.1155/ 2020/8839984.

Neumark-Sztainer, D., Wall, M., Guo, J., Story, M., Haines, J., and Eisenberg, M. (2006) 'Obesity, disordered eating, and eating disorders in a longitudinal study of adolescents: How do dieters fare 5 years later?' *Journal of the American Dietetic Association, 106,* 4, 559–568.

Nolen-Hoeksema, S., Girgus, J. S., and Seligman, M. E. (1986) 'Learned helplessness in children: A longitudinal study of depression, achievement, and explanatory style.' *Journal of Personality and Social Psychology, 51,* 2, 435–542.

Nottinghamshire Healthcare NHS Foundation Trust. (2017) *Mental Health Survey Report for LGBT+ People in Nottinghamshire.* Accessed on 09/07/2021 at https://nottstranshub.files.wordpress.com/2018/07/2017-mental-health-survey-report-for-lgbt-people-in-nottinghamshire.pdf.

Nuttbrock, L., Bockting, W., Rosenblum, A., Hwahng, S., *et al.* (2014) 'Gender abuse, depressive symptoms, and substance use among transgender women: A 3-year prospective study.' *American Journal of Public Health, 104,* 11, 2199–2206.

Oggins, J. and Eichenbaum, J. (2002) 'Engaging transgender substance users in substance use treatment.' *International Journal of Transgenderism, 6,* 1–16.

Owen-Smith, A. A., Gerth, J., Sineath, R. C., Barzilay, J., Becerra-Culqui, T. A., and Getahun, D. (2018) 'Association between gender confirmation treatments and perceived gender congruence, body image satisfaction, and mental health in a cohort of transgender individuals.' *Journal of Sexual Medicine*, 5, 4, 591–600.

PACE (2015) *The RaRE Research Report: LGBandT mental health – risk and resilience explored.* Accessed on 09/07/2021 at www.academia.edu/12165725/The_RaRE_Research_Report_LGB_and_T_Mental_Health_Risk_and_Resilience_Explored.

Payton, N. (2015) 'Feature: The dangers of trans broken arm syndrome.' *Pink News.* Accessed on 09/07/2021 at www.pinknews.co.uk/2015/07/09/feature-the-dangers-of-trans-broken-arm-syndrome.

Pearlman, L. A. and MacIan, P. S. (1995) 'Vicarious traumatization: An empirical study of the effects of trauma work on trauma therapists.' *Professional Psychology: Research and Practice*, 26, 558–565.

Pérez, L. G., Abrams, M. P., López-Martínez, A. E., and Asmundson, G. J. (2012) 'Trauma exposure and health: The role of depressive and hyperarousal symptoms.' *Journal of Traumatic Stress*, 25, 6, 641–648.

Pieritz, K., Schäfer, S. J., Strahler, J., Rief, W., and Euteneur, F. (2017) 'Chronic stress moderates the impact of social exclusion on pain tolerance: An experimental investigation.' *Journal of Pain Research*, 10, 1155–1162.

Porges, S. W and Carter, C. S. (2017) 'Polyvagal Theory and the Social Engagement System: Neurophysiological Bridge Between Connectedness and Breath.' In P. L. Gerbarg, P. R. Muskin, and P. R. Brown (eds) *Complementary and Integrative Treatments in Psychiatric Practice.* Arlington, VA: American Psychiatric Association.

Reese, H. (2011) 'Intrusive thoughts: Normal or not?' *Psychology Today.* Accessed on 09/07/2021 at www.psychologytoday.com/gb/blog/am-i-normal/201110/intrusive-thoughts-normal-or-not.

Reisner, S. L., Pardo, S.T., Gamarel, K. E., White Hughto, J. M., Pardee, D. J., and Keo-Meier, C. L. (2015) 'Substance use to cope with stigma in healthcare among U.S. female-to-male trans masculine adults.' *LGBT Health*, 2, 4,324–332.

Remmers, C. and Zander, T. (2017) 'Why you can't see the forest for the trees when you are anxious: Anxiety impairs intuitive decision making.' *Clinical Psychological Science*, 6, 1, 48–62.

Rhodes, A., Spinazzola, J., and van der Kolk, B.A (2016) 'Yoga for adult women with chronic PTSD: A long-term follow-up study.' *Journal of Alternative and Complementary Medicine, 22*, 3, 189–196.

Ribáry, G., Lajtai, L., Demetrovics, Z., and Maraz, A. (2017) 'Multiplicity: An explorative interview study on personal experiences of people with multiple selves.' *Frontiers in Psychology, 13*, 8, 938.

Roche, J. (2019) *Trans Power: Own Your Gender.* London: Jessica Kingsley Publishers.

Rogers, C. R. (1951) *Client-Centred Therapy: Its Current Practice, Implications and Theory.* San Francisco, CA: Houghton Mifflin.

Rogers, C. R. (1957) 'The necessary and sufficient conditions of therapeutic personality change.' *Journal of Consulting Psychology, 21*, 2, 95–103.

Rogers, C. R. (1959) 'A Theory of Therapy, Personality and Interpersonal Relationships, as Developed in the Client-Centred Framework.' In S. Koch (ed.) *Psychology: A study of a science: Vol. 3. Formulations of the person and the social context.* New York City: McGraw-Hill.

Rogers, C. R. (1961) *On Becoming a Person: A therapist's view of psychotherapy.* San Francisco, CA: Houghton Mifflin.

Rogers, C. R., Stevens, B., Gendlin, E., Shlien, J., and Van Dusen, W. (1967) *Person to Person: The problem of being human: A new trend in psychology.* San Francisco, CA: Houghton Mifflin.

Romero, N., Sanchez, A., and Vazquez, C. (2014) 'Memory biases in remitted depression: The role of negative cognitions at explicit and automatic processing levels.' *Journal of Behavior Therapy and Experimental Psychiatry, 4*, 1, 128–135.

Ross, C. A., Norton, G. R., and Wozney, K. (1989) 'Multiple personality disorder: An analysis of 236 cases.' *Canadian Journal of Psychiatry, 34*, 5, 413–418.

Ryan, E. (2018) 'Intrusive thoughts: How to stop intrusive thoughts.' *MoodSmith.* Accessed on 09/07/2021 at https://moodsmith.com/intrusive-thoughts.

Sakulku, J. (2011) 'The impostor phenomenon.' *The Journal of Behavioral Science, 6,* 1, 75–97.

Sauer, E. M., Anderson, M. Z., Gormley, B., Richmond, C. J., and Preacco, L. (2010) 'Client attachment orientations, working alliances, and responses to therapy: A psychology training clinic study.' *Psychotherapy Research, 20,* 6, 702–711.

Schevers, K. (2021a) 'Ideologically-motivated detransition as a conversion practice: A personal account.' *Ky Schevers blog.* Accessed on 09/07/2021 at https://kyschevers.medium.com/ideologically-motivated-detransition-as-a-conversion-practice-a-personal-account-ee262035453a.

Schevers, K. (2021b) 'Confessions of a Former 'Crypto-TERF.' *Ky Schevers blog.* Accessed on 09/07/2021 at https://kyschevers.medium.com/confessions-of-a-former-crypto-terf-e4ed59d4ec82.

Seebohm, P., Chaudhary, S., Boyce, M., Elkan, R., Avis, M., and Munn-Giddings, C. (2013) 'The contribution of self-help/mutual aid groups to mental well-being.' *Health and Social Care in the Community, 21,* 4, 391–401.

Seligman, E. P., Maier, S. F., and Solomon, R. L. (1971) 'Unpredictable and Uncontrollable Aversive Events.' In F. R. Brush (ed.) *Aversive Conditioning and Learning.* Cambridge: Academic Press.

Selye, H. (1950) 'Stress and the general adaptation syndrome.' *British Medical Journal, 1,* 1383.

Shafran, R., Fairburn, C. G., Robinson, P., and Lask, B. (2004) 'Body checking and its avoidance in eating disorders.' *International Journal of Eating Disorders, 35,* 1, 93–101.

Shaw, C. (2012) 'Harm-minimisation for self-harm.' *Mental Health Today,* 19–21. Accessed on 09/07/2021 at www.careknowledge.com/media/35150/mht-septoct12_pg19-21.pdf.

Siegel, D. J. (2010) *Mindsight: The new science of personal transformation.* New York City: Bantam Dell Pub Group.

Simbar, M., Nazarpour, S., Mirzababaie, M., Emam Hadi, M. A., Tehrani, F. R., and Alavi Majd, H. (2018) 'Quality of life and body image of individuals with gender dysphoria.' *Journal of Sex and Marital Therapy,* 44, 6, 523–532.

Singh, A. (2018) *The Queer and Transgender Resilience Workbook: Skills for Navigating Sexual Orientation and Gender Expression.* Oakland, CA: New Harbinger.

Slade, M., Rennick-Egglestone, S., Blackie, L., Llewellyn-Beardsley, J., *et al.* (2019) 'Post-traumatic growth in mental health recovery: Qualitative study of narratives.' *BMJ Open,* 28, 9, 6.

Snow, M. (2021a) 'Is "Gender Critical feminism" an abuse culture?' *What the Trans!? Blog.* Accessed on 09/07/2021 at www.whatthetrans.com/is-gender-critical-feminism-an-abuse-culture.

Snow, M. (2021b) 'How the UK Government has abused trans people for a year...and tried to look good doing it.' *What the Trans!? Blog.* Accessed on 09/07/2021 at www.whatthetrans.com/the-uk-government-has-abused-trans-people-for-a-year.

Sokol, Y. and Serper, M. (2017) 'Temporal self appraisal and continuous identity: Associations with depression and hopelessness.' *Journal of Affective Disorders* 15, 208, 503–511.

Speegle, T. (2020) 'Laverne Cox tells GMA about her recent attack: "Trans People are in danger... doesn't matter who you are."' *The WOW Report.* Accessed on 09/07/2021 at https://worldofwonder.net/laverne-cox-tells-gma-about-her-recent-attack-the-lives-of-transgender-people-are-in-danger-it-doesnt-matter-who-you-are.

Spradlin, S.E. (2003) *Don't Let Your Emotions Ruin Your Life: How dialectical therapy can put you in control.* Oakland, CA: New Harbinger.

Stamoulos, C., Trepanier, L., Bourkas, S., Bradley, S., *et al.* (2016) 'Psychologists' perceptions of the importance of common factors in psychotherapy for successful treatment outcomes.' *Journal of Psychotherapy Integration,* 26, 3, 300–317.

Stevens, S. (2012) 'Meeting the substance abuse treatment needs of lesbian, bisexual and transgender women: Implications from research to practice.' *Substance Abuse and Rehabilitation,* 3, 1, 27–36.

Stillman, T. F., Baumeister, R. F., Lambert, N. M., Crescioni, A.W., Dewall, C. N., and Fincham, F. D. (2009) 'Alone and without purpose: Life loses meaning following social exclusion.' *Experiential Social Psychology*, 45, 4, 686–694.

Sullivan, M. B., Erb, M., Schmalzl, L., Moonaz, S., Noggle Taylor, J., and Porges, S. W. (2018) 'Yoga therapy and polyvagal theory: The convergence of traditional wisdom and contemporary neuroscience for self-regulation and resilience.' *Frontiers in Human Neuroscience*, 12, 67.

Tabaac, A., Perrin, P. B., and Benotsch, E. G. (2018) 'Discrimination, mental health, and body image among transgender and gender-non-binary individuals: Constructing a multiple mediational path model.' *Journal of Gay and Lesbian Social Services*, 30, 1, 1–16.

Taliaferro, L. A., McMorris, B. J., Rider, G. N., and Eisenberg, M. E. (2019) 'Risk and protective factors for self-harm in a population-based sample of transgender youth.' *Archives of Suicide Research*, 23, 2, 203–221.

Tandoh, R. (2018) *Eat Up: Food, Appetite, and Eating What You Want*. London: Serpent's Tail.

Tang, H. H. Y. and Richardson, R. (2013) 'Reversing the negative psychological sequelae of exclusion: Inclusion is ameliorative but not protective against the aversive consequences of exclusion.' *Emotion*, 13, 1, 139–150.

Tantum, D. and Huband, N. (2009) *Understanding Repeated Self-Injury: A Multidisciplinary Approach*. London: Palgrave Macmillan.

Valentine, V. (2016) *Non-Binary People's Experiences in the UK*. Accessed on 09/07/2021 at www.scottishtrans.org/wp-content/uploads/2016/11/Non-binary-report.pdf.

Van Dam, N. T., van Vught, M. K., Vago, D. R., Schmalzl, L., *et al.* (2018) 'Mind the hype: A critical evaluation and prescriptive agenda for research on mindfulness and meditation.' *Perspectives on Psychological Science*, 13, 1, 36–61.

van der Hart, O., Bolt, H., and van der Kolk, B. A. (2005) 'Memory fragmentation in dissociative identity disorder.' *Journal of Trauma and Dissociation*, 6, 1, 55–70.

van der Kolk, B. A. (1994) 'The body keeps the score: Memory and the evolving psychobiology of posttraumatic stress.' *Harvard Review of Psychiatry, 1,* 5, 253–265.

van der Kolk, B. A. (1997) 'The psychobiology of posttraumatic stress disorder.' *The Journal of Clinical Psychiatry, 58,* 9, 16–24.

van der Kolk, B. A. (2000) 'Posttraumatic stress disorder and the nature of trauma.' *Dialogues in Clinical Neuroscience, 2,* 1, 7–22.

van der Kolk, B. A. and Fisler, R. (1995) 'Dissociation and the fragmentary nature of traumatic memories: Overview and exploratory study.' *Journal of Traumatic Stress, 8,* 4, 502–525.

van der Kolk, B. A., Stone, L., West, J., Rhodes, A., Emerson, D., Suvak, M., and Spinazzola, J. (2014) 'Yoga as an adjunctive treatment for post-traumatic stress disorder: A randomized controlled trial.' *The Journal of Clinical Psychiatry, 75,* 6, 559–565.

van Heugten-Van der Kloet, D., Giesbrecht, T., van Wel, J., Bosker, W. M., *et al.* (2015) 'MDMA, cannabis, and cocaine produce acute dissociative symptoms.' *Psychiatry Research, 228,* 3, 907–912.

Violet, M. (2018) *Yes, You Are Trans Enough: My Transition from Self-Loathing to Self-Love.* London: Jessica Kingsley Publishers.

Vocks, S., Stahn, C., Loenser, K., and Legenbauer, T. (2009) 'Eating and body image disturbances in male-to-female and female-to-male transsexu-als.' *Archives of Sexual Behaviour, 38,* 3, 364–77.

Vollmayr, B. and Gass, P. (2013) 'Learned helplessness: Unique features and translational value of a cognitive depression model.' *Cell Tissue and Research, 354,* 1, 171–178.

Wagner, S., Halmi, K. A., and Maguire, T. V. (1987) 'The sense of personal ineffectiveness in patients with eating disorders: One construct or several?' *International Journal of Eating Disorders, 6,* 4, 495–505.

Walker, D. C., White, E. K., and Srinivasan, V. J. (2018) 'A meta-analysis of the relationships between body checking, body image avoidance, body image dissatisfaction, mood, and disordered eating.' *International Journal of Eating Disorders. 51,* 8, 745–770.

Walker, P. (2003) 'Codependency, Trauma and the Fawn Response.' *Pete Walker, M.A., MFT blog*. Accessed on 09/07/2021 at www.pete-walker.com/codependencyFawnResponse.htm.

Wallace, A. (2018) 'Film and Television.' In C. Burns (ed.) *Trans Britain: Our Journey From the Shadows*. London: Unbound.

Walling, D. P., Goodwin, J. M., and Cole, C. M. (2015) 'Dissociation in a transsexual population.' *Journal of Sex Education and Therapy*, 23, 2, 121–123.

Wang, K. S. and Delgado, M. R. (2021) 'The protective effects of perceived control during repeated exposure to aversive stimuli.' *Frontiers in Neuroscience*, 15, 625816.

Witcomb, G. L., Bouman, W. P., Claes, L., Brewin, N., Crawford, J. R., and Arcelus, J. (2018) 'Levels of depression in transgender people and its predictors: Results of a large matched control study with transgender people accessing clinical services.' *Journal of Affective Disorders*, 1, 235, 308–315.

Yip, T. H. J. and Tse, W. S. (2019) 'Why hope can reduce negative emotion? Could psychosocial resource be the mediator?' *Psychology, Health and Medicine*, 24, 2, 193–206.

Subject Index

Author Index